The In-House Trainer
As Consultant

The Kogan Page Practical Trainer Series

Series Editor: Roger Buckley

PRACTICAL  TRAINER SERIES

KOGAN PAGE

The In-House Trainer As Consultant

KEITH HOLDAWAY   MIKE SAUNDERS

KOGAN PAGE
Published in association with the
Institute of Training and Development

First published in1992

Kogan Page Limited
120 Pentonville Road
London N1 9JN

© Mike Saunders and Keith Holdaway, 1992

British Library Cataloguing in Publication Data

A CIP record of this book is available from the British Library.

ISBN 0 7494 0531 7

Typeset by Koinonia Ltd, Bury
Printed and bound in Great Britain by Biddles Ltd, Guildford and Kings Lynn

Contents

Series Editor's Foreword

Organizations get things done when people do their jobs effectively. To make this happen they need to be well trained. A number of people are likely to be involved in this training: identifying the needs of the organization and of the individual, selecting or designing appropriate training to meet those needs, delivering it and assessing how effective it was. It is not only 'professional' or full-time trainers who are involved in this process; personnel managers, line managers, supervisors and job holders are all likely to have a part to play.

This series has been written for all those who get involved with training in some way or another, whether they are senior personnel managers trying to link the goals of the organization with training needs or job holders who have been given responsibility for training newcomers. Therefore, the series is essentially a practical one which focuses on specific aspects of the training function. This is not to say that the theoretical underpinnings of the practical aspects of training are unimportant. Anyone seriously interested in training is strongly encouraged to look beyond 'what to do' and 'how to do it' and to delve into the areas of why things are done in a particular way.

The authors have been selected because they have considerable practical experience. All have shared, at some time, the same difficulties, frustrations and satisfactions of being involved in training and are now in a position to share with others some helpful and practical guidelines.

In this book, Mike Saunders and Keith Holdaway discuss the role of the trainer as a consultant. This reflects the changing nature of the trainer's function which has come about partly in response to changing organizational needs and partly through the foresight and pro-activity of trainers. Many organizations have come to appreciate that trainers have developed skills that can be applied to a range of activities which involve both organizational and personal development. In consequence, the traditional role of the direct trainer has changed into that of a facilitator, agent for change, communicator and consultant. This change has resulted in a greater degree of specialization for those working in the training and development field.

The specialized role of consultant is not an easy one to move into. This book is a valuable guide to help trainers to establish themselves and the role of consultant to a high level of credibility in any organization.

ROGER BUCKLEY

Preface

Training as a consultancy exercise delivered by individuals as sole proprietors, by small teams or by offshoots of the large management consultancy houses is now enjoying unprecedented popularity. The reasons for
this are only partly to be found in the recession, largely world wide,
experienced as the 1990s began. Of course, the recession meant that
consultants did well as large firms divested themselves of centrally-funded
services with substantial staff complements and overheads, but there are
other things to explain this phenomenon.

Consultancy offers tremendous opportunities to individuals, whether
they are employed full- or part-time, whether retired, self-employed or
even temporarily unemployed. Flexibility of service means flexibility of
delivery. Consultancy can mean more control over what you do and how
and where and when you do it. It is unique in that, like a whole range of
self-employment activities, it offers opportunities for creativity, self-actu-
alization and the realization of personal learning and achievement objectives.

The writers have had experience of consultancy themselves as external
as well as internal consultants. We are firmly convinced that the consultancy role is the way ahead for trainers, who should be able to work in this
way despite the constraints of an established job. It can provide the
flexibility and responsiveness required by the organization as well as
personal satisfaction and growth for the individual.

The benefits to the organization include more focused solutions to
individual problems or needs. Trainers acting as internal consultants
ensure that the knowledge, skill and experience normally deployed and
gained by external consultants remain available within the organization
rather than lost. The consultancy approach can lead to increased job
satisfaction and the retention of experienced staff. It means that business
operations and training services come together while the staff concerned
learn to solve problems jointly. The organization therefore gains added

value from its existing investment in each function.

It is with this firm belief in mind that we have been delighted to offer this contribution in the hope that this sort of development will be further stimulated and advanced.

Acknowledgements

It is in the nature of producing published work that contributions are made by a whole series of individuals, formally and informally. In many cases these are too numerous to mention by name, indeed when material for a particular chapter is discussed, say at an ITD Branch Meeting, an individual comment and the identity of the person making it are not always noted. The authors would therefore like to thank colleagues and associates generally for their contributions and help (sometimes unknowingly) on such occasions.

More specifically we would like to thank, for their key contributions: Anna Beck, Diana Carr, Jenny Eastwood, Sheryl Edgar, John McCann and Michael Walton. We are greatly indebted to these professional practitioners for the insight they have given us into how they worked as in-house training consultants and particularly the procedures, activities and problem-solving with which they are concerned.

We would also like to thank Chrissie Murray who untiringly typed many versions of the manuscript, and Dolores Black from Kogan Page, who first encouraged us to undertake this book.

Finally, we thank our families, especially Lesley and Jane for enduring pieces of paper all over table tops and floors for the seemingly endless period we were working on first and subsequent drafts.

Introduction

Working as, respectively, a tutor and a trainer in a polytechnic and a health authority, we have become increasingly aware of changes within the organization and management of the training function, wherever it is located. Such changes affect the role of the trainer, the shape and nature of training events and activities within the umbrella fabric of a rapidly changing society and economy. The need to package and communicate the significance and application of these changes has obviously arisen. In this book we have sought to explain how the role of internal consultant has become important to the work of the full-time trainer.

We have observed a life cycle within the training function which is almost inevitably followed both by the department and the trainers employed within it. This growth pattern ends with the increased adoption of consultancy styles of working.

Internal Consultancy as a Stage of Development

The organization and delivery of training seems to follow at least four stages of growth and change. Each stage is a necessary reaction to the successes and failures of that preceding it.

Stage 1

An organization does not employ a full-time trainer. Someone, as part of another job, takes responsibility in an administrative sense for processing applications to attend a range of outside training courses. Perhaps one or two types of course or popular centres are chosen and are used in an habitual way. Records are kept by the Personnel Department. Some time later a full-time Training Officer is appointed and takes over these responsibilities. External courses are still used but perhaps needs are now considered more carefully, feedback is received and other types of programme, together with more providers, is discussed. Perhaps costs are examined, reports prepared and recommendations made.

Stage 2

The internal trainer starts to run one or more courses in-house. At first these are informal, perhaps using consultants or managers within the organization.

Stage 3

Some time later, when a comprehensive programme of courses has been built up, an in-house training centre or suite of rooms may come into use. The programme of courses is then reinforced by some training schemes for certain departments perhaps linked to skill-shortage areas. Questions of effectiveness emerge when validation and evaluation studies start to be carried out seriously. This results in 'topping' and 'tailing' activity in which the trainer discusses the objectives and action back at work with the nominating manager before and after the course. Perhaps a briefing sheet is written and a pre-course questionnaire. This helps the delegate work out with the manager what is to be gained from the training, what personal learning objectives there are, how the learning will be applied and what follow-up is required of the manager.

After the course the trainer begins to visit delegates at the workplace, discusses progress and needs with managers, and maybe attends various staff meetings when training questions arise. This stage marks more involvement of nominating managers and an increase in the trainer's influence. It is also characterized by a greater attention to justifying the need for training and linking behaviour to business results. Training becomes integrated into change processes and systems, policies and procedures elsewhere in the organization. It becomes a social process both within and between departments, no longer seen as a discrete activity confined to the training room.

Stage 4

The trainer spends less time personally conducting programmes or even directing them. The trainer's time is spent out and about in the workplace discussing people at work, their performance, their problems and the barriers to behavioural change. The trainer's activity finds a focus on explaining how training can help managers who are now clients. These clients can 'buy' services at the most favourable price. The training is now competing in the internal (and in many cases, the external) market place.

The trainer's role is now less that of a training course provider but a training solution provider, a diagnoser and a resolver. The trainer has become a consultant.

Those familiar with the 'Boston Box' of the Boston Consulting Company will readily see parallels with the product life cycle. The 'Boston Box' graphically illustrates the stages of early development, progressive growth in sales of a product and its contribution to profit generation, maturity and inevitable decline as a result of obsolescence or change in demand. Trainers deliver products. These take time to research and develop, go through periods of popularity, high demand and maybe high-income (actual or notional) generation, before falling into disuse, overtaken by new ideas, materials and approaches. This applies not only to different types of course, but to methods of intervention, training activity, and the changing emphasis between trainer-centred and learner-centred approaches.

It is Stage 4 that this book seeks to explore, explain and discuss.

Design of the Book

Most of our readers will be familiar with Kolb's well-tried model of the experiential learning process, and many trainers will apply the principles explicitly or implicitly in the design of their own training and learning.

In essence, the model suggests that training takes place through a series of intellectual and behavioural stages operating in succession. Experience in a concrete or pragmatic sense is a prime source of learning. When we reflect on that experience we may 'see the light of day'. There can be no learning unless we make sense of what we experience, perhaps by making connections between that and other experiences including stored memory and images. From then on new behaviours resulting from this 'digestive' stage will lead, or can lead, to new experiences and the cycle is complete.

We have tried to apply this model by structuring each chapter as follows:

- The process is started by providing information by discussion, illustration, theory input or model.
- Reflection is prompted by questions and case studies designed to stimulate thinking and transfer to the workplace.
- Active experimentation and concrete experience is provided by a 'Programme of Action' designed to encourage the reader to try things out practically (possibly in between reading each chapter).

Chapter Format

To achieve what we have described, each chapter starts with a summary and a list of competency objectives as a target for learning. This is followed by the input or models for that particular chapter. There follow some simple and outline applications by way of example. A more detailed case study continues throughout the book (see below) to elaborate the theme for the chapter. We ask questions to encourage reflection about the concepts and the practice described.

Finally, the 'Programme of Action' provides suggestions for tasks for the reader to carry out. It suggests how to extend the reader's current work and how to go on building on the contents of the chapter.

Three Extended Case Studies

To make transference easier we have also used extended case studies. We have chosen three fictional situations (but drawn from life) to illustrate how the themes and contents given in this book may work out or are working out in practice. We have 'serialized' episodes from one case study at the end of each chapter to illustrate the various aspects of the consultancy process described. The other two case studies have been included as Appendices. We offer these as additional examples of in-house consultancy in practice, to highlight many of the problems and differences in style which may be encountered. We pose some questions to help readers relate the main themes of the case studies to those developed in the book.

The three case studies are concerned with:

- A voluntary sector association.
- A District Health Authority.
- An electrical goods manufacturing company.

We hope that this approach will help to breathe life into the principles and theories described while helping to draw out new thinking and insights and to stimulate learning and action.

Case Study

Now meet the subject of our extended case study, Liz Clarke, Senior Training Officer, National Association for the Welfare of Young People (NAWYP). Liz works for a national body in the voluntary sector at its national headquarters in Birmingham.

She has been with her current employer for about three years and in her current post for eighteen months. Her first appointment to NAWYP was as a Field Trainer in the Association's south-west region, spending a lot of her time setting up local workshops, administering national schemes at regional level such as a limited number of Open Learning packages and college programmes together with a whole range of 'boring' tasks (her word) like signing trainees' expenses claims.

She moved to Birmingham on promotion to work as a Management Trainer in the HQ Training Department. Here, her work included overall responsibility for the Management I and Management II programmes. The first was a three-week junior management course which the Association had been trying to provide centrally for the small regions and locally for the large regions through Regional Trainers and colleges or other providers. The idea had been, when these arrangements were first put in hand a few months ago, to standardize first-level formal management training provision as much as possible.

The second, more recent programme consisted of a range of short three- to five-day courses, on various management topics considered to be appropriate to the needs of middle grade managers throughout the organization. In this case an attempt had been made to go beyond the 'across the board' approach by seeking to provide items of input and practice which in some rational sense corresponded to needs of managers. Thus most people in the appropriate grade would expect to attend the Management of Time workshop but not all would get Case and Project Management; all would attend Practical Communication but only some Statistics for Managers and so on.

The Headquarters Training Department lists 8 staff in all: the Training Manager Jean Wright, two management trainers, two technical or specialist trainers and secretarial staff.

With the Personnel Department the Training Department is part of the Human Resource group, one of the Head Office functions, each of which provides services within the central establishment as well as on a functional basis to Regional staffs.

1 Role of the Trainer

▷   S U M M A R Y   ◁

In this initial chapter we explain some basic points for practising as a consultant in-house.

1. We mention the role and contribution of training as an activity within the organization, about which every trainer must be clear as it affects each workplace.
2. We briefly examine forces and factors influencing the part the trainer can play both now and in the future.
3. We explain more practically how a trainer can apply some of these ideas to personal work in order to pave the way towards implementing and developing a consultancy activity.

After reading this chapter and working through the prescribed tasks and suggested applications you should be able to:

- understand the current and future role of the trainer
- identify core competences
- analyze your personal role and determine an optimum effective role for a client situation
- actively negotiate and gain agreement to that role.

The Organization's Need for Training

All organizations have objectives, some explicit, some implicit. Objectives can be at a variety of levels from corporate or strategic, to operational or first level. Senior managers and those at the higher levels of the organization constantly seek to ensure objectives are compatible at the various levels and the work of individuals, sections, departments and divisions is coordinated to a planned outcome. Such is the task, process and responsibility of corporate management.

To achieve objectives work is done, tasks are carried out and members of the organization perform. Objectives are expressed in policies again down through levels in hierarchical fashion, to guide and suggest how people should perform. Plans show in a detailed way how objectives through policies can be translated into activities within the bounds of who does what and when.

Again, these are the instruments by which coordinated effort is achieved and decisions concerning alternative courses of action are made. Obviously different departments' functions will have their own objectives, policies and plans but ideally these will contribute to and enable the more general business objectives, policies and plans to be achieved.

Training as a function and as a set of activities is concerned with improving or changing behaviour. Behaviour means, in a work context, performance. It is often said that training can influence skills, knowledge and attitude-change or modification. Thus training objectives are concerned with helping people perform according to what is required so that they contribute adequately, directly or indirectly to what the organization sets out to achieve.

It is important for us to remind ourselves constantly of what training may be able to achieve and certainly what it may not be able (or is extremely unlikely) to achieve. It can only be justified as a legitimate business activity in the terms described above. It is most closely related to changing human performance. It cannot contribute properly to organizational objectives except in this way.

Let us pause for a moment and think about this quite simple but highly significant idea.

REFLECTIVE QUESTION 1.1

What is the importance of linking training policies and plans to business policies and plans?

Training, Performance and Change

One of the ideas we hear talked about very widely when organizations and their success is discussed, is change. Organizations, we are told, must change their ideas, their products, their structures and their philosophies or go under. The fashionable term is transformation. How is this to be achieved? Achieve it we must if continuity and survival let alone growth are to happen. We return to objectives. These can be drawn up for the current situation and the future situation, both the possible future and the likely future. Whatever the case a key ingredient will be the degree to which human beings can perform differently, more or better maybe, but certainly in some way not as they have done in the past. All sorts of influences affect the need for change whether in human terms or in structural ones. From this we can safely assume that training as a function will never cease to be desirable as a way by which a deliberate attempt can be made to modify behaviour.

We cannot see the trainer (or the training function) becoming in an objective sense redundant. By degrees and in some situations, a few individuals may be able to change themselves, adapt their attitudes, improve existing skills, acquire new skills and add to their knowledge. This taking responsibility for one's own learning is a powerful step towards self-development. But it depends on the ability of the individual and not all are able in this respect. Also it depends on motivation. Again this is a quality which influences different people to do different things – not always what those influenced by the resulting actions would wish.

A simple equation we have found useful as trainers is that of performance as a function of motivation and ability, written as:

$$P \int M * A$$

Many other factors of course influence the likelihood of desired performance. A place to perform and the wherewithal, like resources of various kinds, are all essential. Much of this is a matter of management action. Trainers are interested in ability and motivation, as these are factors that, once diagnosed properly in relation to a training need, represent something that training can do something about.

How many of us know of people with lots of motivation, keen and interested in the work to be done but with no apparent ability to perform? Equally the reverse: lots of ability defeated by lack of or loss of interest, apathy and perhaps laziness, symptoms of low motivation? The everyday phrase 'ready, willing and able' neatly sums up the point.

As change demands new and different performance so new abilities and motivation will be called into account. The trainer's contribution is for the present and the future; it changes and adapts through time.

What Type of Trainer?

The role of the trainer, the part the trainer is called on to play, has been fairly extensively researched and publicized. Primarily the trainer has been seen as a course provider, a programme director, a training material designer and developer. All these roles or sub-roles are summed up as 'direct' training. But this doesn't just happen by chance. Roles become explicit and get written into specifications and descriptions as a result of history, experience and maybe a kind of folklore of expectations by users which has been gradually built up. We see this by looking at the role set, the people-colleagues, customers, suppliers, consumers, seniors and juniors, who influence our roles as trainers or are influenced by us in turn. Nothing is static in a change of events, happenings and stirrings which influence and cause to change structures, policies, the nature and shape of the work people do.

From being a direct trainer a myriad of other role possibilities present themselves. These may be adviser, specialist or expert, facilitator (at a variety of levels) entrepreneurial 'make it happen' agent and many others. A thought to consider is that behind these developments will be some basic skills and knowhow that will be expected of the trainer. These include such things as identifying training needs, writing training objectives, designing and running training events of various kinds, using key methods, and handling various types of audio-visual aids. Such core competences become the tools of the trade of the professional trainer and form the central context of professional training received. This is similar to the accountant who qualifies in the essential principles and techniques of accountancy but who later specializes in one area, such as taxation, or becomes a management consultant. This is a little less clear for trainers because training as a function, particularly in its latter-day guise as Human Resource Development (HRD), has only recently emerged (and is continuing to emerge) in the same recognizable manner.

Analyse your own role, using the following checklist:

1. What is the source material for your role, eg job description, 'contract' at selection interview, etc?
2. What are the four or five key activities, tasks and objectives you see in your role, assumed or made explicit to you?
3. What roles would you say you have? Think of nouns signifying roles such as those ending in -er or -or.
4. What are the influencing factors affecting these roles and which reinforce expectations of others, eg. inherited work or objectives?

Some of these questions may be easy to answer, some less so. But, as with all the tasks and questions, we want to encourage you to seek out answers by active enquiry. You may come across unclear areas, cases of no information, or even blank stares. But as we shall see, in order to explore and apply the role of consultant, the in-house trainer needs to establish a starting point as well as the nature and context of training expectations and demands which pertain on the personal doorstep.

REFLECTIVE QUESTION 1.2

How far have you thought about your role as a trainer? Do you think it is something generally known and understood by those around you or does it need to be made explicit? Does it need to be changed now?

Case Study

When Liz applied for the post in Birmingham, she was sent a job description plus some details about the background of the post, the work of the training department up to that point and the future policy and likely developments. The emphasis as she saw it was to rationalize the provision of management training at least on a formal basis of off-the-job training. Nothing else of substance was mentioned except 'to investigate the efficiency and effectiveness of the present and immediate future situation and methods of delivery and to make recommendations to ensure that both needs and objectives are met'.

There was some discussion at the interview and later with Jean Wright in the first week of taking up the job. From these interchanges it emerged that the two-level approach had been the pet idea of Jean herself when running the training department single-handed. What had then happened was the agreement of the Establishment Board to a post to take over this work as a result, no doubt, of some good spadework by Jean.

If asked she would probably see her role as course provider and as course developer.

Recently some changes have been taking place, possibly not all of them equally welcome. Numbers of nominees for courses seem to be dropping, although from staffing figures the need for people to attend, at least on a theoretical basis, seems to exist. Why should this be?

Talking to various people Liz has found that although individuals say that they think the courses are important and worthwhile they simply:

1. 'do not have time to attend'
2. 'are now under a lot of pressure to cut costs'
3. 'are rethinking their priorities'.

In other respects there has been some good feedback. One or two managers who have sent some of their staff on centrally provided courses have started to ring up to ask about developments to course content. There has been at least one call to ask Liz for advice about a training matter. What seems to be happening is that managers are looking for some changes more in line with how they are now seeing the situation.

Yesterday Jean asked Liz in for a chat. The general run of her thoughts were as follows:

1. The Association is developing from the Board downwards a 'Strategy for the mid-1990s and beyond'.
2. A new mission statement is being drafted reflecting changes in government policy and an enhanced image reflective of changes within the Association and the society it serves.
3. Training must move with the times. Training must be measurable, meet people's needs, deliver the goods. Managerial roles and how they are structured and acted out as well as the formal pattern of organization, must match and reinforce these changes.
4. Culture and climate should promote the objectives of the Association and training should contribute wherever possible.

Pondering on these points, the conclusion Liz reaches that evening as a result of talking to Pat, her flatmate, is that her training interventions will need in future to be more flexible, more in line with people's changing or current expectations, certainly as far as possible linked to results which will benefit the Association:

PAT: But, Liz, are you going to be in a difficult situation? On the one hand you are trying to follow the official line, the classic top down approach. On the other you want to be flexible to each manager, all of whom probably see things differently and have their own agenda and political slant.

LIZ: Yes, I can see what you mean. But perhaps once I have gained credibility as a trainer who can help with individual problems, who is seen as someone who can get down to brass tacks...

PAT: There is certainly a dilemma here but you have to start somewhere. How about picking up on some of the positive feedback you have got already. If Jim Broadhurst wants your help with his office staff training go and see him. It doesn't mean going behind your boss's back. I don't see why at the same time you can't carry on with what you have been doing up to now, at least for the time being. After all, you can build the new policy line into the programme and make sure that the official side is covered by the normal memo or whatever.

LIZ: I'm sure you are right. It has to be the way forward but it just feels too *ad hoc* for my liking and all a bit too untidy. But if I can make a go of this it gets me away from the same old trainer role. That is not what I think training is really about or certainly not what it is all about. Maybe what I need is a ...

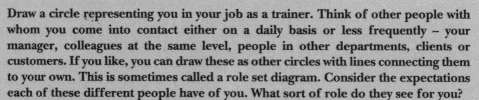

▶ PROGRAMME OF ACTION ◀

Draw a circle representing you in your job as a trainer. Think of other people with whom you come into contact either on a daily basis or less frequently – your manager, colleagues at the same level, people in other departments, clients or customers. If you like, you can draw these as other circles with lines connecting them to your own. This is sometimes called a role set diagram. Consider the expectations each of these different people have of you. What sort of role do they see for you?

Think about the activities that are associated with these roles and how these activities contribute to your own objectives and in turn to the objectives of the business as a whole. Perhaps you will discover some contradictions or inconsistencies.

Complete the diagram and discuss with your manager. As an alternative, fix it to your office wall and get views and comments from visitors.

2 Current Changes

> SUMMARY ◁

1. We look briefly at the training function and how it has developed, and the current challenges faced by trainers in an increasingly harsh economic environment.
2. We show how these developments give the in-house consultant a key training role.
3. We indicate how these trends are further reinforced by changes and institutions in the wider environment, e.g. the increasing emphasis everywhere on work-based competency.

After reading this chapter and working through the prescribed tasks and suggested applications you should be able to:

- interpret the current environment within which the training function operates and understand how the trend towards the use of a consultancy approach to training is moving
- identify the rationale for the consultancy approach
- start to develop and apply the internal consultancy approach within your personal situation.

For the trainer these trends represent both problem and opportunity, both challenge and confronting issue. Here is a situation brought about by natural developments in the way training is delivered together with changing, and increasingly articulate, demands and expectations of clients.

We hope that if you accept these premises this chapter will provide you with the means of accepting this role and also with a framework for applying it to your own work situation.

The Training Function and How It Has Developed

The training function refers to that part of the organization concerned with the execution of staff training. This means people and their activities, their resources and the delivery of services developed. The training function in the UK today is largely a product of the 1964 Industrial Training Act. This linked the levy/grant system to the appointment of a full-time training officer in many situations where no such person had been employed before. Trainers were appointed, in many cases, to justify their positions by optimizing the amount of grant received in exchange for the levy made on a particular company. Side by side with the appointment of trainers was the implementation of what came to be called the 'systematic approach to training'. This involved identifying training needs, often across the whole organization, developing training initiatives to meet those needs, then systematically validating and evaluating the results against the objectives set.'

Before the 1964 Act, trainers were employed in some traditional manufacturing areas, especially in various aspects of engineering and production, and also with the (then) public utilities – gas, coal, electricity and the like. Often these appointments were part of the statutory obligation to train built into the legislation that established such national monopolies. In many instances the trainer was appointed as a technical instructor and was often an ex-craftworker. In others the trainer was the apprentice-minder where apprenticeships represented the only evidence of systematic, formally instituted and properly organized training.

One of the consequences of the Act was to make the trainer an administrator and, in some instances, he or she had to take on the role and trappings of office manager and part-accountant. This was occasioned by the form-filling, the compilation of statistics, the record keeping and rendering of returns required by the levy/grant procedures. In the UK the 1978 Training of Trainers Committee established by the Manpower Services Commission (MSC) of the time investigated the role of the trainer. They identified four role 'elements'. These four – direct training, planning and organizing, determining or managing, and consulting and advising – subsequently became the basis for a good deal of trainer training. Indeed almost until the present time the four elements have been used as a way of profiling individual competence when assessing for the Institute of Training and Development's (ITD) Certificate in Training and Development.

A more varied pattern has since emerged, or perhaps a more realistic view of what trainers actually did as part of their daily work. This development resulted from a growing body of training technology and the appearance of new techniques which revitalized training methods and spawned new sub-specialisms.

Objective evidence is provided by any of the recent publications issued by the professional training bodies. Peruse the advertisements and you will see specialist services covering every conceivable aspect of training management and delivery.

Training Today

As we entered the 1990s most sectors of the world economy were gripped directly or indirectly with recession. Low growth, stubborn inflation, and in some areas innovation inertia combined to place enormous pressures on employers generally, on budgets all round and on training departments. With the pressure on resources where training was seen as a cost rather than an investment, deep cuts were seen as an unavoidable response. The result has been a demand on the training function to produce short-term outcomes, and an increasing emphasis on quantifiable evaluation.

In the UK a tension has arisen in which we have seen cuts and shortages on the one hand and exhortations on the other, to make up skill shortages identified as delaying economic development and causing the country to lag behind its international competitors. Investment in training is seen as a necessity, but investment can be made only when an upturn in business generates income to finance that investment.

The Growth of Consultancy

A further phenomenon has been the growth of the consultancy profession, especially in terms of small business and sole proprietors. At the same time we have seen redundancies in perhaps unprecedented numbers. Are these two phenomena related? It is cheaper for an organization to employ a consultant to run a Job Instruction Workshop or an Equal Opportunities three-day course at say £300 or £400 a day, rather than keep permanent staff in established posts to do the same thing. Or so runs the rationale of the accountants.

This type of development is well in line with Professor Charles Handy's 'shamrock organization'. In this model of future organization he suggests the three leaves are composed of a core of full-time workers, a second group of part-time workers (possibly working at home) and a final group of contract workers. These would include consultant trainers, some of whom might be ex-full-time employees of the same parent organization. It is an interesting way to retain the services of people who have learned the ways of your organization without incurring the high overheads of employing them all the time. At the same time you get the benefit of the experience and ideas those staff consultants are gaining from working with other clients.

REFLECTIVE QUESTION 2.1

How is my organization changing in terms of patterns of work and employment?

As well as the flexibility that the use of outside consultants brings, there are likely to be different uses of full-time trainers as well. Some may have flexible contracts, meaning some work on other projects or for other people within the organization, becoming part-time in that sense. More and more of these trainers may be appointed on a short-term renewable contract basis.

Better use of in-house facilities may mean getting other people to use your rooms or training materials, or to buy places on your training courses.

REFLECTIVE QUESTION 2.2

What methods can I use to produce a commercial justification for the training I organize or deliver?

Alternative Approaches to Training Delivery

The conventional course, as many of us understand it, is fast disappearing. Alternative approaches to delivering training go hand in hand with increasing emphasis on accurately diagnosed needs. The normal training model at its simplest is in three parts (see Figure 2.1).

Figure 2.1 *The normal training model*

Preparation

This includes identifying needs, design of the training intervention and administration.

Training intervention

This covers how the learning objectives are met. The training intervention design, its content and methods.

De-briefing

This is the validation and evaluation process. It includes any follow up and reinforcement activity in the workplace.

Alternative approaches can be built on to any one of these three stages or components (see Figures 2.2–4)

Preparation

Activities extend into the workplace. Training preparation moves into operational work and business meetings.

Pre-course questionaires		
preparation	training intervention	de-briefing
managerial briefings		

Figure 2.2 *Building on alternative approaches: preparation*

Training intervention

A whole range of new and innovative approaches are available and are being developed. These range from a wide variety of indirect (as opposed to face-to-face methods) to self-directed programmes, opportunistic learning through learning contracts and many others.

Pre-course questionaires	Indirect methods	
preparation	training intervention	de-briefing
managerial briefings	self-directed programmes	

Figure 2.3 *Building on alternative approaches: training intervention*

De-briefing

This may be extended into increasingly sophisticated evaluation models in addition to follow-up workshops, application studies, research projects and further training.

Pre-course questionaires	Indirect methods	quantitative measurement
preparation	training intervention	de-briefing
managerial briefings	self-directed programmes	application studies

Figure 2.4 *Building on alternative approaches: de-briefing*

As training methodologies develop and the means of delivery become more varied, the role of the trainer can become splintered. As it splinters there is room for the growth of specialist options and specialist contributors. As will become apparent, these specialists can be external consultants. Equally the situation offers opportunities for the in-house trainer as a consultant.

The contribution of the trainer is no longer limited to the training room or centre. Different options and alternative methods of resolving training issues spark off ad hoc approaches which lead to an issue-focused consultancy role. For example, an information technology (IT) trainer in a large company in the hotel and catering industry provided training services to constituent divisions in the group. The consultancy role developed from an initial central course provided as a guide to management on their IT opportunities. This meant becoming increasingly involved in the business objectives and plans of a manager as client.

Training and the Line Manager

For a long time the line manager's role in training has been emphasized as being of critical importance. The traditional view has been that the line manager sets the standards governing the work done and staff performance. He or she should therefore be closely involved, directly or indirectly in the training which is carried out to influence behaviour synonymous with or related to those standards.

The integrated approach means a trainer is adviser rather than executive. This is a further trigger prompting a consultancy role. There is also a link to training development (product life cycle idea) given in the Introduction.

Macro-environmental Changes

With increasing pressure on trainers to deliver cost-effective training, the value of which can be demonstrated and quantified, emphasis has been placed on competence outcomes. For example, in the UK during the early 1980s a highlight of the Government's Youth Training Scheme was the analysis of generic families of jobs eg, receptionist duties. This produced groups of common core skills with defined competency standards. The skills of dealing with office paperwork or acting as customer receptionist were dealt with as a series of individual items. Once competence was achieved it was reasonable to suppose that the experience and achievement were transferable from one job to another. Skills ownership and skills portability would motivate individuals and help competent employees respond to changing and variable job opportunities. This whole process, as far as the United Kingdom is concerned, has been formalized by making evidence of competence essential to obtaining a licensed qualification endorsed by the National Council for Vocational Qualifications (NCVQ). The NCVQ approves courses which are designed to produce observable competence and use assessment methods which look for competent performance as direct evidence of a satisfactory standard. Other moves in this direction are the Industry Lead Bodies which are groups of managers and specialists representing a particular industry or professional area of work. These bodies have produced or are producing statements of competence as standards to be achieved by those providers of education and training in that particular area.

For trainers, the Training & Development Lead Body has produced a whole list of competences for trainers which will be enshrined in courses and training provided nationally. Included in this list are tasks and sub-tasks, elements and range indicators to enable training and performance to be geared to one-off local situations but, at the same time, to fit acceptably into an approved national framework.

For our purposes the emphasis on competence means not only that the trainer is required to have consultancy skills, but also that consultancy is a way of achieving competence by effective delivery of the product and service.

> ### REFLECTIVE QUESTION 2.3
>
> What are the opportunities potentially open to me arising from the competency-based approach?

The Change Process

In the 1960s and 1970s it became fashionable to speak of the trainer as an agent of change. This was associated with what was then seen as an exciting new development, promising all sorts of new role opportunities for trainers. Such was Organization Development (OD). Emphasis could be on individual knowledge and skills enhancement, but this was to be rapidly extended to groups and teams, then to departments and the organization as a whole. On the way training would encompass changes in methods, procedures and systems to encompass 'across the board' change essential for organizational health and continuity. Later the approach was identified in a more general sense as the management of change associated with a whole array of 'systematic approaches' and 'culture shift' mechanisms to implement it.

Change means often a fundamental self-appraisal by the individual as the basic building block of change. This concept has led to an emphasis on interpersonal skills training and various types of awareness-arousing approaches. Changes in training philosophy, methods and approach have been manifested in the learner-centred approach from which have sprung self-development, self-directed and self-managed learning. The glue pulling all the components together has been learning contracts, jointly-agreed (manager and staff member) learning objectives, personal development plans and portfolio evidence of achievement. These have been devices to bring together learning and work, new behaviour and better performance, increased skill and increased work-related effectiveness. As already pointed out, all these processes and developments have come together to underscore and underpin the concept of vocational competency.

Case Study

A day or two later Liz is in Jim Broadhurst's office. He tells her that he has a number of office staff who, he feels, need some 'training'. They tend to be erratic in their performance, some of them come in late in the mornings and one or two cause 'more than a bit of a problem'. Jim has three supervisors, two of whom recently attended the management course which was held mainly for staff from the North West Region. He wanted all these supervisors as junior managers to motivate and develop their staff to perform better and at a more consistent and satisfactory level.

JIM: 'I'm a bit disappointed in the course I must tell you. At first I had high hopes but these people don't seem to have learned anything. Or if they have it's not helping me in this department.'
LIZ: 'I'm sorry to hear you say this and that you feel this way. Can I do something to help? Maybe I could have a chat with the supervisors or attend one of your meetings?'
JIM: 'Well I did have something like that in mind. But I'm not sure what you need to do. It may be something I need to do, or the supervisors ... or all of us together'.

Subsequently Liz and Jim agreed some rules which would govern any collaborative work they might engage in. Any training activity which takes place will as far as possible:

- be geared to meet defined needs;
- have a measurable pay-off in terms of Jim's own objectives and will be defined in the same terms as Jim's work is judged;
- will involve both the line manager and trainer.

Jim is anxious that his staff are properly motivated at all levels. This provided Liz with the opportunity to suggest the importance of involving people and trying to get them to identify a benefit from learning and changing. She is also able to link Jim's concern for training which really does deliver, with the whole concept of tailored training designed to meet the needs of the workplace. This naturally leads her on to her concept of competency which, in turn, will probably line up with the organization's strategic intentions.

Liz summed up where she had reached: Jim was receptive to her doing some work for him and being involved in it himself; they had agreed some ground rules and some principles which could be used for planning and monitoring; but she felt uncertain about the exact nature of her role which was yet to emerge.

► PROGRAMME OF ACTION ◄

Review of last chapter's activity

In Chapter 1 the overall role of the trainer was put forward and discussed. In Chapter 2 we have moved on to see how the internal consultant role has come to the fore, why it is important and how you can go about putting this information and concept to work for you in order to increase the competitive position of yourself as a trainer and the effectiveness of your organization.

Action for this chapter

List pressures on you to deliver training and whence the pressures come. Against the items indicate activities or tasks needed to satisfy stakeholders and constituents.

Compare these tasks and activities with priority areas identified as critical in your own situation, eg objectives given by your manager, items arising from your last appraisal.

Draw up a matrix showing current and future activities against the methods or roles adopted for them. Show how the consultancy role will/could emerge to meet new and changing expectations. Make notes on how links could be made between external changes affecting your industry or area of work and the adoption of a consultancy style. These changes might be shifts in demand for products or services or the activities of Industry Lead Bodies establishing standards and competences.

3 What Do Consultants Do?

> ◁ **SUMMARY** ▷

1. We discuss the role of external consultants in terms of their clients' expectations and look at the pressures this creates.
2. We examine the activities of consultants in terms of their style and the resources they bring to the client and how those activities vary through the different phases of a project.
3. We describe different types of situations where consultants are used.

After reading through this chapter and carrying out the suggested activities you should be able to:

- agree the role of an external training consultant with managers and the consultants employed
- optimize your use of external consultants by knowing the advantages and disadvantages of their use.

Role of the Consultant

As we have seen, a role is largely a set of behaviours played out by someone in accordance with what they think the situation demands – or, alternatively, with what they think people expect of them. In much the same way we can look at consultants, management consultants, training consultants, almost any kind of consultant.

Consultants are very much in the business of trying to meet the expectations of their clients. Why do you think this is so? Well, clearly consultants stand or fall according to the extent that they are credible, that the people hiring them, paying them and using their services have *confidence* in them.

If it is so important for consultants to be perceived favourably by their clients in order to be successful we then move on to some more questions. How do consultants know what clients or potential clients expect? How can they deliver or communicate the message (expectation) in an acceptable way? After all, the consultant may not always want to go along with the expectation of the client, but rather seek to change that expectation, knowing it will be better for a more likely successful outcome to a particular project.

A Simple Example

A training consultant is talking on the telephone to a potential client, the Training Manager of a light engineering company. The Training Manager wants someone to 'sort out' the training of the first-line supervisors. 'We want someone who knows what they are about to get our guys to stand up for themselves and give orders properly. We don't want supervisors who leave it wide open for people to take out grievances or who spend all day chewing the fat over personal hang-ups,' he says. 'Well,' he goes on, 'I've got people like you knocking on my door every day, what can you offer me?'

The trainer's thoughts are: I could probably get and deliver the job. I might be effective in the short term, but what about later on? Do I want to meet the perception of the client as it stands or seek to change it? Do I take the job and to hell with it? (My manager has expectations of me, as well.)

What analysis would you make of this situation in throwing light on the role of the consultant? Here are some pointers which might help:

- The client wants a 'fix-it' person (possibly to get rid of a problem someone is pressing him about).
- The client has probably diagnosed the issue incorrectly, perhaps on the basis of an isolated incident without thinking of wider issues.
- The right solution needs to be linked to the right problem or issue.

Who are Consultants?

Consultants are found everywhere, not only in the traditional professions, but also in new areas every day. Being a consultant means providing a type of service in a given field. Sherlock Holmes called himself a 'consulting detective'. Clients consulted him on the basis of his acquired knowledge, skill and experience. He combined all the essentials of the modern consultant – expert, advice giver, action taker and a resource, whether physical or mental. He also, like most consultants, worked for a fee, except that in his case the fee never varied except when he chose to waive it completely. In another respect he resembled other consultants. People paid for his time as much as for his practical services. Time was always pressing for him and he often negotiated a set amount of time perhaps regardless of a guaranteed outcome. Dr Watson as a General Practitioner was also a sort of consultant (although in the medical world the term is usually reserved for those at the upper end of their profession!).

What Do Consultants Do?

Consultants are sources of expert advice and an extra pair of hands. They provide services of analysis and identification, of problem-solving, of issue clarification, of information and action. Their contributions are specialized and developed from a particular type of in-depth knowledge or advanced skill. They are often employed on a short-term basis where permanently employed staff have neither the ability nor perhaps the time to carry out the same work.

Avoidance of Responsibility

Consultants, particularly management consultants (and training consultants as a sub-group) have suffered in the past from negative media images based on all sorts of stereotypes, perhaps because they have been seen as efficiency experts or interlopers called in to take unpopular courses of action without taking proper responsibility for the consequences. Typical comments concern the consultant as someone who 'borrows your watch to tell you the time and then keeps the watch'. The consultant 'tells you something you already know'; 'spends time asking question, never giving answers'; is a 'failed practitioner who now tells others how to do it'. The feeling of escaping responsibility seems to be at the root of these sentiments. Some of this may be fair comment, but much of it is not. There are many instances in a whole realm of different situations, including training and development, where an external consultant has been very beneficially employed.

> ### REFLECTIVE QUESTION 3.1
>
> What are your perceptions and images of consultants?

Going back to the key point of the consultant being in the business of meeting expectations of clients; to stay in that business we can perhaps say that the role of the consultant is above all to act as a resource. This means a resource for information (consultant as expert), a resource for facilitation (consultant as problem identifier, clarifier and analyst) and a resource for performance (consultant as practitioner, implementer and action-taker).

Activities of External Consultants

Activities are closely related to roles (see Figure 3.1). Activities show how the role is translated into practice.

Role of external consultant	Resource to Manager	Overall Purpose
Expert	Information	
Problem identifier		To
clarifier	Facilitation	meet
analyst		expectations
Practitioner		of
implementer	Performance	clients
action taker		

Figure 3.1 *Relating activities to roles*

Activities

The activities in turn encompass logical stages of development concerned with entering into a particular assignment, collecting the necessary data and carrying out the work needing to be done. These stages can conveniently be seen as gaining entry and agreement, research, implementation and disengagement.

Gaining entry and agreement

This is the opening stage of a consultancy project or assignment. It will include the initial contact between the consultant and the client. Here the problem or opportunity can be outlined. The consultant listens, asks questions, makes some preliminary notes. This is an exploratory stage during which the basis of a possible contract can be worked out, possible options identified, varying courses of action put forward and mutual trust developed. The consultant may wish shortly afterwards to put initial thoughts on paper as the basis of a proposal. An agreement may emerge leading to the written contract which will establish aims and objectives, forward strategy and methods, what will be delivered, when and at what cost. Some consultants, especially those with a narrower band of 'products', such as those offering certain types of training courses, will use a standard proposal letter in which specific details can be inserted.

We have to remember of course, the consultant's prime concern is with cost and time. These often amount in the consultant's mind to the same thing. The consultant has to collect enough material about the problem or opportunity to put forward a *credible* proposal, bearing in mind the need to meet the client's expectations. However, the contract might not be secured, in which case a cost has been incurred to no avail, except perhaps in terms of publicity and marketing experience. Once a contract has been negotiated and agreed, the next stage is research.

Research

This is the second stage. Now information can be collected from a variety of printed sources and through meetings, discussions and interviews. A written questionnaire might be used. The research helps the original objective to be teased out and reviewed and perhaps, if the terms allow, the contract to be changed. As we have seen, the client's perception of the problem or issue may be inaccurate. This provides an opportunity to clarify such questions. Symptoms and causes may have become confused and it might be important for the consultant in the role of analyser and clarifier to point this out. In so doing, options and alternatives, consequences and implications can be set out. This is a useful contribution. The client is often too close to the situation to see all aspects of it that are much more readily apparent to the outsider. Research then is data gathering, feedback and review by discussion or consideration.

Sometimes of course the consultant's job may finish with a report at this stage. This will depend on what was agreed at the start and the nature of the original commission. If not, the third stage will be entered into.

Implementation

Here final proposals can be put into action. An example might be when a training need has been established arising from a performance discrepancy or shortfall observed over a period of time. The consultant has been called in and has clarified the issue and made suggestions on various courses of action. A training intervention is considered suitable and the go-ahead to its design is agreed.

At all stages the consultant will report back on material collected, see individuals, attend meetings, submit plans and proposals. The client may be involved in an administrative capacity, helping to set up meetings, make crucial decisions or in carrying out parallel activity.

The external consultant may look on a consultancy project as being at the level of one or more individuals, a particular group, a set of groups or a whole organization. In clarifying the extent of the project it will be important to ascertain those involved. Various conventions and assumptions are at issue here. These will include defining who owns the problem (if any), who needs to be consulted, who possesses the information and who has to act on the results. In other words, this is a 'map' of the stakeholders, the human forces at work which will make or mar a successful outcome.

Disengagement

After carrying out a piece of work for a client, either research or implementing solutions, the final stage is a formal period of disengagement. Its purpose is to:

1. Evaluate the results of the activity
2. Help make the changes stick
3. Establish the nature of any continuing relationship between consultant and client.

The consultant works with the client to reassess the objectives and the extent to which they have been achieved. This may involve discussions or a summary report. It will usually indicate further work to establish or 'refreeze' the advances made. It is legitimate for the consultant to propose further work he or she can do but this is often seen as covering up a poor job in the first place and needs to be done with care.

Some consultants by chance or by design, create a dependency on themselves which is not healthy for the client or ultimately for the consultant.

Closing events or short ceremonies such as a presentation to, or by, staff who have been involved in the changes are often an effective way to close a project and disengage.

This phase of an assignment is important and frequently overlooked. Failure to close properly can undo a lot of good work.

Activities covering the four phases of project negotiation and execution are summarized in Figure 3.2.

Stages	Activities
Gaining Entry	Building trust, listening, exploring preliminary noting and issue identifying.
and Agreement	Contracting, negotiating, defining limits, establishing aims and objectives, clarifying, questioning, listening.
Research	Gathering data, interviewing, planning the way ahead, presenting and reporting, analyzing and sifting, proposing options and alternatives.
Implementation	Carrying out training action, evaluating, putting into practice the agreed proposal.
Disengagement	Stabilizing, evaluating and reinforcing progress, final reports, identifying future action.

Figure 3.2   *The four phases of project negotiation and execution*

Why Organizations use Consultants

Responsible people in organizations use consultants for a variety of reasons. We have to think back to the roles of consultants and the activities they engage in to understand fully why this is so. One thing we can say is that consultants are being used more and more by all sectors of employment, private, public and voluntary. At least two important reasons suggest that this trend will continue.

Consultancy Specialization

First, the consultancy business is becoming more and more differentiated. At one level we find the large prestigious firms often offering management as well as training consultancy services. These are often offshoots of accountancy, engineering or other types of professional services. Training consultancy can be seen as related to a mainline consultancy service in a particular specialized area. At the other extreme is the freelancer. There are many in this category. Possibly we are talking of someone doing training consultancy on a part-time or full-time basis, sometimes in association with other work, or as someone recently retired or made redundant. In between there are partnerships or loose associations of people working from home or perhaps a small office over a High Street shop. This differentiation of providers caters for different types of client or business. It is difficult to say whether the market came before the growth in the number of providers or the other way round. Certainly many more people are now using consultants for their training work than would have been the case even five years ago.

Contracting Out Services

Second, more and more work that would previously have been carried out internally is being contracted out. This has the advantage of cutting down on expensive employee overheads and also allows short term contracts to be negotiated which allow for fluctuating economic conditions while avoiding 'casualty' costs like relocation, restructuring and redundancy. This provides an economic context for the use of consultants. It can be highly cost-effective.

Consultants can be called upon to work on a variety of projects, at differing levels, as we have seen, and for different periods of time. Herein lies the great attraction of flexibility.

A consultant can be hired for his or her expertise to come in, weigh up a situation then *prescribe* a remedy by recommending a course of action. The consultant is a professional accountable for the quality of that recommendation. Once given, the consultant's responsibility is over. The client can act on the recommendation or not. The consultant can also be retained, ie kept on to implement the recommended course of action. An alternative is to use a consultant to *challenge* a situation letting in a cold breath of air from outside, so to speak. This may be a perturbation factor to help the organization and its members, alone or with help, confront the demands in a situation of change and thence to manage that change successfully. The consultant may be used to *confirm* a conclusion reached by management or perhaps just as a *catalyst* helping the client by oiling the wheels of the system so that it copes with a problem or issue a little better than it would have done unaided.

Some Examples

Case studies used as part of a polytechnic's Diploma in Training Management course illustrate how and why certain organizations may use consultants.

Two of these situations concern mythical metropolitan administrations whose Training Departments approach firms of training consultants with a request for help. In one case it is to put forward proposals for a series of middle-management training courses and in the other for a programme of team building and team development events. The training consultants are represented by students while the clients are the tutors to the Diploma course. The consultants interview the clients, collect data, put forward interim and final reports, present proposals and make quotations to carry out a consultancy project. Various reasons can emerge for the use of consultants by these clients such as certain departments being publicly seen to be taking action, or for reasons of the individual status and prestige of a particular manager. All reasons of this type are mixed in with ostensible reasons such as best use of resources, harnessing specialist expertise, use of outside resource for flexibility and economy.

The other two case studies are a little different. In one, a cooperative specializing in energy-saving services and products, the consultant is seen as a problem identifier and clarifier in a situation of internal rivalry and competing factions. The consultant is at risk of being 'set up to fail' in order to build up one individual's personal power-base. 'I called in consultants because you wanted outside advice. Now look what's happened. I told you so. If you had listened to me in the first place this wouldn't have happened.'

In the final case, an insurance company wants help with its equal opportunities policy including a possible implementation programme. Is the use of consultants being made so that the company can appear publicly to be socially responsible? Is it to avoid the cost of Industrial Tribunal adverse decisions? Is it to improve its staff relations? Or what?

Why an organization wants to use consultants may be obvious. Equally it may be a question near the top of the list at the early stage of consultant-client contact. It may be seen as affecting the relationship fundamentally as well as all subsequent stages of project negotiation, planning and implementation.

Getting the Best Out of the Relationship

Working with a consultant may offer the trainer a good deal of useful experience as well as knowledge. In so doing, a flexible-looking agreement can be drawn up showing how the two will work together: who will do what. You can vary your amount of control and involvement.

Consultants are likely to be experts. Using consultants is a good way of tapping up-to-date experience, knowledge and expertise. This may be more cost effective than developing the same thing internally. Their experience of delivery may mean they can package the offer in a credible way if a presentation is made to senior management. The credibility of the consultant is at stake here as well as the Training Department.

REFLECTIVE QUESTION 3.2

What are the implications of using outside consultants for my own role as a trainer?

So Why Use Them?

The key advantage in using consultants seems to be that they have to produce results to survive. The pressure is on them to do a good job. The client's commitment is for the contracted period only. Afterwards you need not re-hire. You can learn from the experience and take your business elsewhere.

Consultants as outsiders are expected to be objective and not take sides. This is often why they are used, that is, as political neutrals. Not only this characteristic of objectivity but also the ability to look at issues in a wider context must be advantageous. The consultant draws on parallel situations and experience of other assignments to look globally at your organization.

There is always another viewpoint. An advantage is only an advantage if it is perceived in this way by the client, and this depends in turn on a whole set of local and environmental circumstances. In appreciating fully the advantages and disadvantages of using an outside consultant, singly or in combination with the trainer as internal consultant, we need to look at what internal consultancy really means. We return to this theme later.

Case Study

Liz has taken the opportunity presented by a chance remark, to check with her manager about NAWYP's experience of using outside consultants. She gathers that in the recent past there has been some initial training to coincide with and to help implement a new quality assurance policy. Another project was concerned with the implementation of a particular and popular brand of team work and team building training. She is interested in reactions to the use of outsiders by managers and other staff. This could colour how Jim Broadhurst and his staff will regard her efforts as a kind of insider-outsider.

JIM: 'Well I suppose I would see you as an expert of some sort but also as someone who can take a job off my shoulders, save me a lot of time and hopefully do a better job than I could.'

LIZ: 'But you're an expert as well ...'

JIM: 'Yes, but not necessarily the same as you in this case. After all you're the one who has had the relevant training or you wouldn't be in this job!'

LIZ: 'I ought to say that I think my role is spending time in your department working *with* you as well as *for* you as you put it.'

Bit by bit the role was thrashed out, not entirely to her satisfaction, but well enough to provide an agreement governing how Liz will work over the next week or two.

Already the principles previously agreed were coming in handy as a reference and a yardstick – much more than she had expected.

▶ PROGRAMME OF ACTION ◀

Review of last chapter's action
If you plotted the diagram of styles of working versus key areas of work you will probably have noticed that you work differently with various members of staff or in particular types of assignment. The expectations of different clients and the pressures they exert, require different methods and outcomes. You might also have identifed instances where it would be appropriate to change to a consultancy style.

Action for this chapter
Examine your organization's previous use of consultants. List how they were approached and how they were chosen. Where did the impetus come from, who proposed their use? What sort of brief was given, did it change, was the project a success? How can you tell?

4 Consultancy within the Organization

▷ SUMMARY ◁

1. We move on from consultancy in general to the internal training consultant in particular.
2. To reach this point we examine some of the differences in contribution and position between the insider and the outsider, while focusing on some of the important similarities as well.
3. We consider how the internal trainer can reap the benefits of the consultancy approach and go about gaining acceptance of this role.
4. We explore the likely implications if the consultancy approach succeeds and continues.

After reading this chapter and working through the suggested tasks and applications, you should be able to:

- understand the nature and context of the internal consultancy role
- list the potential benefits to be gained from acting as an internal consultant
- know some ways and means of gaining organizational acceptance of the role
- see the short-, medium- and long-term perspectives and implications of the internal consultancy activity.

REFLECTIVE QUESTIONS 4.1–2

What are the attitudes towards consultants of principal and influential decision makers in your organization, and what are the implications of these attitudes?

How would these perceptions affect how they see – or do not see – your role as a consultant working internally?

What In-house Consultants Have To Offer

As a consultant you must be seen as having something to offer: credibility as a person and as a specialist. Perhaps you cannot offer what is traditionally associated with the outsider and what the external consultant offers: the objective view, the different perspective, the apolitical status; but you can and should offer consultancy skills and a consultancy approach to service delivery.

Having said this, the following characteristics of the external consultant should also apply to the internal consultant:

- Professional approach
- Specialist in own field
- Able to relate to people at different levels
- Impartial.

The internal consultant is likely to be knowledgeable not only in a particular field of industry or employment, but in the products, services and day-to-day working of a particular organization. As a permanent employee, probably full-time, even if relatively new in that particular position, the consultant will enjoy a degree of acceptance. Any work that is done, data built up and experience acquired is a net gain for that organization. This is not just a question of a record or report being made or produced. Rather it is experience and skill that is added to the composite bag of skills and experiences of the organization's workforce as a whole. By acquiring the experience the individual has acquired it for the organization. Unless that experience is hermetically sealed within the trainer, which is virtually impossible, much of this 'intellectual property' becomes part of the organization's sum total of resource.

Whatever is gained as a result of the internal consultancy becomes much more of a long-term asset which is not 'lost' to the organization; it has become imperceptibly part of it. It does not stand out as somehow 'foreign' and as a one-off special study or investigation, but is something that is now embedded and which is much more likely to be used again and again and to be linked to other future activities.

Other benefits of the trainer as internal consultant are:

- Different forms (as well as level) of costing mean more projects may be considered practicable than was originally thought.
- Saving of briefing time, 'getting to know', induction and settling in; and reputations are 'on the line'. This is similar to the case of the external consultant but with one important difference. The external consultant goes away with a good or bad reputation in the

context of a big pool. The internal consultant carries the reputation around every day in close contact with the original users and clients, the detractors and critics as well as the supporters.

- Ability to see the 'warts and all' wider picture.

It is worth remembering that the internal consultant can always call on the services of the outsider for assistance, whether it be on a practical basis, such as producing training material or running a training event, or whether in a more passive sense, as a sounding board. The difference will be that the internal trainer is managing the assignment and accepting accountability for its successful conclusion.

Agreeing the Role

This is a key aspect. Our roles can constantly change as part of the shift of external events and pressures. Trainers tend to adopt a consultancy style of working in response to a particular set of these pressures. On a general basis, as we discussed in the Introduction, the training function itself can be seen to mature from an administrative system through analysis and in-house teaching to more outreach work, which often culminates in a consultancy service.

Individuals also react to changes within their job, perhaps a reorganization of the department, or moving to another company with a different style of working. Trainers might also adopt a consultancy style in response to specific assignments or projects within their job where this is most appropriate.

Whatever the spur, altering one's style of working has multiple implications for the organization, work colleagues and trainers themselves. Unravelling these types of interaction is frequently the sort of work that many trainer/consultants are asked to take on in their new role so that the process involved (as described below) can be seen as a mini case study in itself.

It may be that aspects of the consultancy role will creep in 'by the back door' and resulting activities and work patterns become gradually established as the norm. This may cause no surprises and no raised eyebrows. Equally, in structured types of training organization with clearly delineated roles, expectations may mean that a change of approach and type of work by the trainer is noticed and perhaps opposed! As an extreme case, if the trainer is seen as 'course provider' and then stops providing courses and instead spends time seeing managers and individual staff members for consultations and discussions there may be ensuing problems.

The trainer can be proactive and not be carried along by events. This means predicting what the demands on the training function are likely to be in the coming six months to one year period and how they can be best met. It means that if traditional direct training and training administration work is not going to continue, people know about it. Those affected must also see for themselves how their needs can be met. Others may want to satisfy themselves that what is being done is likely to meet the objectives contained within any published training policy or plan.

It is useful to examine systematically the perceptions of those likely to be influenced by a consultancy assignment. After all it is an intervention and is always going to lead to a change affecting all sorts of people directly or indirectly. Two commonly used approaches which can be employed at various levels of sophistication are role set analysis and stakeholder analysis. The first, which we looked at in Chapter 1, looks at people whose role impinges on or is affected by activities of the key role. In this situation it could be the client or manager originating the issue giving rise to the consultancy assignment. These people may be peers, seniors, staff within the organization, suppliers, consumers and others outside it. Stakeholder analysis particularly refers to those who have a personal stake – financial, reputation, own work activity – in the success of a particular project or the specifics of a particular outcome.

In each case we need to think of what people's objectives are and what their expectations are likely to be in terms of inputs and methods. Are these expectations likely to change? What sort of previous experiences have people had to shape these expectations?

It may not just be necessary to publish what the training approach is going to be hereafter. It may be necessary to negotiate to a point of agreement, especially with the trainer's manager. This will mean being clear in your mind what you want to achieve and how you intend going about it. Obviously things can change by degrees in terms of introducing and applying the consultancy approach. Various stages of implementation – identifying the issue, clarifying the objective, agreeing the contract, project management, review and disengagement – can be built up gradually. For example, minor issues can perhaps be worked through quickly to build confidence in oneself and one's own abilities as well giving the client confidence in the consultant. In this case project management might amount to a little desk work and one or two meetings. Short-term assignments of this kind will be excellent practice grounds and help substantiate the consultancy role more formally.

Alternative Aspects of Consultancy

The trainer's consultancy role may be one of adviser, helper, provider, facilitator or one of a dozen or more possibilities. These are dealt with in greater detail in later chapters. The trainer might initially work through some of these possibilities in order to gain confidence and experience, and to awaken in the client growing awareness of what can be achieved. Being an active adviser may be a preliminary stage, followed by a passive advisory role associated with a more pronounced listening rather than a 'telling' style.

Pay-offs

These readily break down into those associated with short- and longer-term results. Short-term results will probably be practical and task-related, akin to conventional expectations of training delivery. In the longer term there will be results associated with process issues – the nature and function of Human Resource Development (HRD), individual roles and self-perception. Concepts such as managing personal learning and turning insights into action plans may be relevant. Overall there will be issues of organizational change and renewal as well as growth and development.

Training Policy

There is a link between changes in the shape and culture of an organization and of its training department. Documents (such as policy statements and job descriptions, missions and plans) which were drawn up in response to one set of conditions should not be irrevocable and should not be allowed to act as a barrier to change. We do not intend to argue the merits or de-merits of any particular purpose or statement for training. However, the espoused purpose of the training function within an organization will strongly influence people's expectations and the decision making that goes on within the function. Clearly if the purpose of the training department is defined as:

> 'to provide a programme of training courses for staff based on the expressed needs of the company's managers'

the expectation is that the department will be course-centred, probably operating with a large staff of instructors in a specific training centre. Another statement of purpose might be:

> 'to assist managers identify the training needs of members of their staff and implement training solutions'.

This suggests a greater involvement with managers, providing an expert service and probably running training programmes based around individuals.

A third definition:

> 'to contribute to profitability by helping to develop the capabilities and attitudes in the workforce which enable it to perform effectively'

emphasizes the link between training activity and profitability and the effect on the workforce as a whole rather than individuals. This last definition leaves the way open for the adoption of a consultancy style. Any document which sets out to define the purpose of training within an organization must represent the views of the stakeholders rather than a largely unsupported statement of ideals, however 'high'. It would be unwise to rewrite the definition of training purpose simply to fit in with a new 'more modern' style of training activity such as a consultancy approach. Managers will simply ignore it. It is far better to hold discussions with managers from all levels to find out what is needed and what is acceptable within the broad spectrum of possibilities you can offer. This may come, as already indicated, as part of a deliberately planned process to move from a conventional direct trainer role to an internal consultancy one. Alternatively it may result from a period when consultancy work is proceeding side-by-side with other training work and the need arises to clarify and agree the way ahead for the training function. In this case, the path and process may be easier once the client has become attuned to the consultancy approach and ethos. The involvement process becomes just another part of the consultancy role at work.

REFLECTIVE QUESTION 4.3

What is preventing the acceptance of my role as a consultant? What can I do to change this?

Organizational Implications

We have used Galbraith's model of organizations to help to explain and describe the implications of adopting a consultancy style throughout the organization. This emphasizes the degree of 'fit' between the five constituent parts of any organization:

1. Work/tasks
2. Structures
3. Information and decision processes
4. Reward processes
5. Human resources

and the way in which the organization frames strategies and objectives in response to demands from the environment.

1. Work/Tasks

Clearly the type of work to be undertaken by the training department will change. There will be a shift in emphasis away from a programme of course provision towards working on the shop floor with individual managers.

2. Structures

It may be necessary to change the structure of the training department to reflect new work patterns. A shift from hierarchical to project team or matrix working may be useful. These considerations are really only important to large departments. One issue is the place of a training consultancy within a Personnel Department. Opinions are divided. Some trainers wish to distance themselves from the personnel function to reduce the perception of managers that they are 'working for someone else'. Others feel that the Personnel Department is such a rich source of information, money and influence that it is counter-productive to leave.

3. Information and decision making processes

Changes may need to be made in the types of records kept. Whereas in the past attendance at training events may have accurately reflected the activity of a department, it may be necessary to collect data such as manager contact time or staff time spent on particular projects. Critical decisions may have to be taken regarding where to work and how much resource to devote to particular projects.

4. Reward processes

Intrinsic rewards and job motivation will change. Not all trainers will get the same satisfaction helping managers to train their staff as doing the face-to-face training themselves. This is an important issue for trainers who are excellent presenters and who know that they could lead the session better. They have to learn to let go of their previous expertise and start doing things where they feel unsure. If adequate alternative rewards are not identified and forthcoming it is only a matter of time before the trainer reverts to old, comfortable ways of doing things. Merit payments, bonus schemes or other performance-related pay which may be part of a trainer's salary must be linked to the new parts of the role being adopted.

5. Human resources

The staff involved in this work will need to emphasize or develop different aspects of their skill repertoire. Interpersonal skills of listening, persuasion and analysis will be required to an unusually high degree.

Consultancy styles of working may be better suited to part-time, flexitime or job-sharing workers. Staff may be conveniently based at home or work from a remote site since access by large numbers of course participants will not be needed.

In Conclusion

There are clearly wide ramifications to the decision to adopt a consultancy style as an in-house trainer. In the following chapters we examine all these aspects in some detail and in the final chapter indulge in some speculation as to where it all might lead.

Case Study

The role is negotiated and agreed: Liz will seek to clarify the issue or problem as originally posed by Jim and having agreed it with him, will suggest the way ahead in terms of interventions or actions required. Liz will guide and prompt so that a positive use is made of agreed criteria. She will keep the project on path as a kind of 'process' or 'systems' person as well as taking on any training required as a 'task' person.

Liz has opened a file on the assignment and carefully keeps a record of her discussions with Jim and on what they both agree. She feels reasonably happy about the way things are going but has some niggling concerns. Everything seems to take much longer to discuss than she thought. The more you seek to discuss and obtain agreement the more the whole process seems to drag out. People's expectations can be raised when their opinion is sought – they are flattered and pleased to have their thoughts and feelings taken into account. Liz is anxious that they will become impatient and be looking for results before she is ready. There have already been some heavy hints about how long it is all taking; people don't for a minute consider that they may be the cause of the delay!

Liz is also convinced that Jim still regards her as some technical wizard with some clever or esoteric solution up her sleeve, ready to be produced like a genie when the moment is ripe. While on the subject of Jim, Liz is not convinced that he has accepted his role as responsible manager, to commit himself to taking action at the proper time to bring about something worthwhile.

'Oh! And there are lots of other things that don't bear thinking about. Everyone is expecting me to deliver the goods on time, and what about Jean's lecture ...'

> PROGRAMME OF ACTION ◀

Review of last chapter's action
In Chapter 3 we suggested that you look at your organization's experience of using consultants of any sort. This raised questions of selection, briefing, introduction and review of the subsequent work undertaken and the results achieved. What learning can be drawn from this review?

One or more of these conclusions may have emerged:

- Consultants are often chosen by a key decision-maker based on ascribed credibility. This may be, in many instances, based on powerful associations with prestige, a name, a product or even a logo.
- Consultants may be 'in the family': 'we always use JT Services', 'National Head Office use them', 'they have a reputation within our industry for knowing about our industry'.
- Consultants were selected on the basis of a small bit of telling evidence, key words and phrases, used by a reputable competitor.

Action for this chapter
Consider your current objectives as a trainer and the means/activities used to achieve them. Consider how far this arrangement is satisfactory, now and in the future, to meet likely demands and changes. Consider the stages in transition from a non-consultancy to, say, an 80 per cent consultancy role. What would be the stages in transition to achieve this and how could the various stages of a consultancy assignment be introduced, albeit on a small, short-term scale to facilitate this?

List potential benefits of the internal consultancy role in relation to your current situation. Use a grid indicating the 'now' and the 'future' situation.

5 Starting an Internal Consultancy Service and Securing Contracts

$\triangleright$ SUMMARY $\triangleleft$

1. We shall concentrate on those skills and techniques useful in developing relationships with clients ('gaining entry'), securing agreements to carry out work and the pre-diagnostic phase of any consultation assignment or project.
2. We show how an individual needs to look at his or her personal abilities and situation in order to develop a strategy for changing to a new method.

After reading through this chapter and carrying out the suggested applications you should be able to:

- analyse your own situation and plan how to start working in a consultancy mode
- start to build a working relationship with clients
- write costed proposals for action.

The reasons or pressures for changing to a consultancy style of working should be identified so that a sound rationale can be put together, even if only to answer those people who ask, 'Yes, but *why* are you changing …?' Having a clear reason for making the change will help the trainer/ consultant overcome any new difficulties, stay with the new style and resist the temptation to return to old methods.

The Politics

There are some practical considerations about whose decision it should be to alter the style of working of individual trainers. Clearly the job holder needs to be enthusiastic about the change and must be able to persuade his or her manager to go along with it. This could be one of the early tests of using influencing skills! Other legitimate stakeholders in the decision are the senior management team or board, client managers and colleagues within the training and personnel function. Communicating your intentions and managing their reactions and expectations will be looked at below when we look at communication techniques. Be practical however. If 'The Board' hasn't involved itself greatly in training affairs in the past it is unlikely to do so now. As a colleague of ours says, 'It's easier to get forgiveness than permission.'

REFLECTIVE QUESTION 5.1

How can you encourage people to come knocking on your door?

Planning How To Start

Personal SWOT

(Strengths, Weaknesses, Opportunities and Threats.) One commonly used method for developing strategies and action plans is to carry out a 'SWOT' analysis. Individuals or groups are asked to identify and write down a list of their strengths and weaknesses. These might be considered the internal resources and limitations to actions. The next stage is to look outside their function and identify the opportunities open to them and the possible threats they face. A possible example of such an analysis for an internal trainer moving into a consultancy mode is shown in Figure 5.1.

Having carried out this exercise, the findings are turned into an action plan by asking:

- 'How can I maximize the opportunities?'
- 'How can I reduce or avoid the threats?'
- 'How can I reduce my weaknesses?'
- 'How can I build on my strengths?'

Using this technique, Figure 5.1 might be developed into a list of actions such as the following:

1. Informal lobbying and discussion with managers.
2. Produce a target list of interventions based on the operational plan for the coming year.
3. Try a few pilot schemes with friendly managers. Build the use of in-house training into designs to safeguard the training centre.

STRENGTHS
- Good knowledge of training methods.
- Good track record with most managers.
- Solid programme of courses to refer to.
- Decisive and persuasive.
- Good Learner.
- Boss's general support.
- I want to do this!
- Computer literate.
- Numerate.

WEAKNESSES
- Lack of experience in this style.
- No real links with Finance Dept or dealing with very senior managers.
- Impetuous on occasions.
- Evaluative rather than empathetic listener.
- Unsure about exactly how I will do this.
- Project management skills.
- Weak links into the Board.
- Reliance of managers on off-job courses.
- Training not tied into business needs.

OPPORTUNITIES
- Have greater impact on organization's performance.
- Chance to work with Finance.
- Personal development and growth.
- Greater ability to direct effort where it will have most effect.
- More responsive to changing needs.
- Become more businesslike.
- Chance of work outside company.

THREATS
- No clients.
- Closure of training department.
- Loss of accommodation and course provisions.
- Loss of department budget.
- Extra paperwork and contracts.
- Wasted time touting for business.
- Conflicts of agendas (mine and theirs).
- Loss of bonus associated with course take-up.
- Less training going on.
- Rejection of method by managers.

Figure 5.1 *A typical SWOT analysis for a trainer moving to a consultancy style of working*

4. Practise active listening skills – get structured feedback from clients/colleagues.
5. Spread the word of success to raise other expectations of managers.
6. Attend course on project management.
7. Carry out costings exercise on consultancy time.
8. Identify a project with Finance and carry it out. Renegotiate bonus scheme payments away from course attendances towards results at work.
9. Cultivate links with Director of Personnel – offer to progress one of his/her pet projects.
10. Review use of training centre.
11. Offer to delegate training budgets to departmental managers following analysis of training needs.
12. Form a careful plan of all this to manage self and avoid rash decisions.

Making Contact

If as a trainer you do not already have a list of target interventions in your head you are unlikely yet to be in a position to work in a consultancy mode. Being established within the organization and talking to managers, trainers are bombarded with evidence of problems to tackle. Working with course participants is a rich source of information about situations which need to be followed up, although the trainer must *always* respect the confidentiality of discussions with such people. The best way is to ask the participant (usually at the end of the day) if an intervention would be welcome.

People with whom we have discussed initial contacts have all said something to the effect that 'you just have to be brash, pick up the phone and ask for an appointment'. Being genuinely concerned about the individuals involved and the effective functioning of the organization makes these approaches feel quite natural.

Having access to hard data is very important. Managers are more receptive to approaches which are based on solid evidence of performance weaknesses than general enquiries asking if they need any help. Being part of the Personnel Department helps here since it is usually the source of rich data on say, turnover rates, exit interview results or skill shortage figures.

Acting as an internal consultant could cut off the supply of information to any individual who seeks to cast off old ties.

Board Presentations

High profile presentations to the Board or groups of managers are a high risk strategy which can produce rich rewards in terms of managerial commitment. However if they don't bite, the consultant can lose a lot of credibility. Approaches to individual managers are a safer way to start; but do trainers always want to be safe? Some internal trainers advertise their consultancy service through leaflets or other literature about the Training Department. Usually this starts out as a statement that 'all courses can be tailored to individual departments' or an offer to work with managers to design specific training solutions. Only the very largest organizations seem to produce glossy brochures comparable to the major consultancy firms.

After Contact is Established

Probably the key skill of working in a consultancy style is listening. 'Really listening' we shall call it through this chapter. Most trainers pride themselves on their listening skills, and many teach them; but how often do we deploy such skills with rigour, self discipline and very hard work? 'Really listening' is demanding and tiring. When done well it provides the listener with a clear understanding of what has been said and some empathy with the feelings of the client and demonstrates to the client that this has happened.

One of the main benefits of really listening (being involved in the discussion without passing judgement or leading the client) is that the client also gains a much clearer understanding both of the situation and his or her own feelings. Many problems at work are cleared up in this way with no further intervention from the consultant. Such discussions are powerful shapers of events and can lead to clients solving their own problems. This leaves the consultant aware that he has helped but unable often to claim any credit!

Ownership by the Client

This brings us to re-emphasize an important point. A successful intervention inevitably feels owned by the client and his staff; without this ownership it would not stay in place after the consultant leaves. This means that most credit for success must rest with the client, not with the consultant. Trainers who cannot, or will not, live with this situation either tend to build up a dependency on themselves or stick to giving short-term expert advice. In our opinion the second is the better option. We shall examine below, in the sections on proposals and marketing the service, how to obtain the most from such situations. Enough to say here that sound review meetings or reports, built into the project, can serve to emphasize the consultant's role.

What Are We Trying to Achieve?

There are five aims of listening to keep in mind during discussions with clients:

1. To gain a full understanding of what is being said and of what is being described.
2. To discover and empathize with the speaker's feelings.
3. To encourage the speaker to be full and frank.
4. To discover and confront your own feelings about the client and the situation.

5. To contribute towards building a trusting relationship between client and consultant.

Clearly these are all interlinked, especially 3 and 5, but any of the particular listening behaviours or techniques described below will contribute to each to a greater or lesser extent.

Preparation for the discussion

Self-preparation before a meeting can help understanding enormously. By familiarizing yourself with the client's background, business aims and key relationships, you can avoid interrupting the client with questions of clarification on such basic points. This also increases the client's perception you as professional and hard-working, which contributes to building the relationship.

The second part of preparation involves constructing a model or overall scheme of the information required to feel confident that the entire situation has been covered. We used Galbraith's five point model in Chapter 4 to describe the consultant's role in the organization. This and other models can be useful to both parties to structure explanations and questions during explanatory discussions.

It is important not to jump to conclusions during this preparation and it should not lead to the stripping of preliminary explorations during discussion with the client. Such behaviour suggests that the consultant has his or her own agenda, probably to implement another client's project rather than to help them!

During the discussion

Early discussions between the consultant and client are usually fact finding and confidence building. It is therefore important not to influence the client or to bias the description he or she gives of what is happening, perhaps in trying overly to please or impress the consultant.

To obtain an accurate description, the listener should try to act as a mirror, reflecting back to the speaker his understanding of the situation and the feelings involved. Some people fall into the 'tape recorder trap'. They try to be non-directive by just recording what is said with minimal input beyond vigorous nodding of the head and visceral grunts of encouragement. This is as exciting, and as interesting, for the speaker as talking into a malfunctioning dictaphone! The consultant has to be actively involved in discussion. The knack is to ensure that all the ground is covered by directing the conversation without introducing bias into what is being said.

We describe specific listening behaviours in the following chapter (page 82) and suggest ways in which they may be developed and improved.

Keeping notes

Summarizing at regular intervals what has been explained is a key skill to develop during all discussions with clients. A proforma sheet such as that shown in Figure 5.2 will be of use to ensure all the details are included. Having a dedicated sheet in this way also makes the project file easier to follow and avoids all kinds of scraps of paper finding their way in.

Meeting Notes	File No. xx		
Participants	Contact No.		
Time and venue:			
Main points:		Action Who	When
Page ___ of ___			

Figure 5.2 *A suggested proforma for keeping meeting notes*

Being Persuasive

The client's view of the situation may be very different from that of the consultant. People disagree with one another for any of four reasons: they may have different information, different objectives, or different values. Alternatively, one or both of them may be mistaken.

Internal consultants frequently find that they have to persuade clients or clients' colleagues to alter their behaviour or expressed opinions (attitudes) around particular work problems. It is important when working with clients that you both share the same views, objectives and values around the project if later arguments and misunderstandings are to be avoided. These misunderstandings arise when client and consultant find themselves diverging in what they are trying to achieve.

Disconfirmation

We have discussed above the 'listening route' to a shared understanding. There are often occasions when the consultant believes that the client has got things wrong or is avoiding difficult issues. The process of changing the client's view relies on disconfirmation. This is the process of making the client feel uneasy, perhaps a little anxious as a result of continuing to hold their view in the face of new information or experience relating to their beliefs. This process is shown diagrammatically in Figure 5.3.

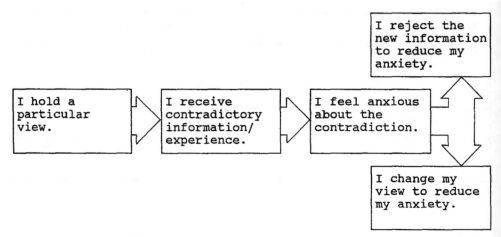

Figure 5.3 *The stages in disconfirmation, altering one's views*

As an internal consultant you must make a judgement about how much anxiety you will be required to generate to bring about a change. Some individuals will be very open-minded and willing to change their views with little pressure.

This process has been described by many authors as unfreezing, movement or changing, and refreezing. It applies both to individuals and groups (or organizations) and is the basis of much thinking on organizational development.

A. J. P. Taylor once described himself as 'a man of extreme views weakly held'. This illustrates that extremeness of view should not necessarily deter the influencer (although you should be very careful!).

If the views are close to the client's core values they will be extremely difficult to shift and it may well not be worth the effort for the job in hand.

The consultant must shift too

Being persuasive is a worse than useless skill if you are wrong: it is positively damaging. Part of mature persuasion is constantly to check one's own position and understanding and being willing to shift towards the client's position.

Pushing and pulling

If you push against someone they stiffen up and push back to maintain their position. The same kind of reaction occurs in conversations, where one person tries to convince another by force of argument, personality or authority. An internal consultant frequently lacks corporate authority over a client and does not have access to usable incentives or sanctions. Pushing clients to change their view is tiring and not very rewarding work.

Pulling clients through a problem or, better still, exploring it together, tends to produce less resistance since the value of their current position is recognized and the consultant seeks to move them forward into new situations. Clients can be steered to confront possible future difficulties by careful questioning. This should enable them to discover possible benefits and nasties for themselves. This realization, when it occurs, is often clear to see on clients' faces, 'the penny drops', and a certain determination to act starts to develop.

PUSHING	I apply sanctions	
	I tell you what I want	Increasingly consultant centred
	I tell you how I think	
	I tell you what I feel	
	I identify what we have in common	
	I tell you what may happen	Increasingly client centred
	I question	
	I listen	
PULLING	I disclose about myself and my situation	

Figure 5.4 *Pushing and pulling*

Kindling the Fires

What follows is like building a flame from a smouldering tinder. A client's ideas need to be fanned and encouraged, explored and built upon. Kindling has to be added until the client's flames of commitment can withstand burial under a large quantity of hard work! This is an exciting process and can lead both client and consultant to get carried away in the first flush of enthusiasm. Such excitement is one of the reasons why so many projects start without a thorough diagnosis of the situation and without the costs, probability of success and likely benefits of the project being properly identified.

Confronting situations

Confronting clients is a painful, generally unproductive exercise. Our experience is that it is best avoided.

Working with clients to get them to confront their own inappropriate behaviours or unhelpful (or simply incorrect) beliefs about situations is, however, central to the work of a consultant. We would go so far as to say that often little helpful progress can be made without it.

Despite such sage advice, at the time it often feels like a person-to-person conflict and it usually feels rather uncomfortable. As consultant you need to feel good about yourself and the client, confident that your own observations are true and are both useful and relevant to the client. These are the core of good feedback skills.

Assertiveness

Standard assertiveness techniques are valuable here. We do not intend to go into detail in this book on such methods. Useful references are listed in the bibliography.

The Relationship Between Client and Consultant

The nature of this relationship varies according to the nature of the assignment, the expertise of the people involved and the stage reached in the work. Figure 5.4 summarizes how the consultant's role varies according to the relative expertise and inclination to become involved. Where you, as the consultant, are completely expert in the subject you should simply do the job. Where the client is expert and keen you are best advised to do nothing and find a job where you are needed. Between these is a whole range of behaviours moving from active listening, through interpretation, building a vision, identifying options, making recommendations and simply telling the client what to do.

Record Keeping

Keeping notes during meetings, especially while summarizing, is extremely valuable. It can help to demonstrate progress during the discussion and provides a valuable gauge of how well the consultant has understood the situation during a review. Chaotic, unintelligible notes are a sure sign that the position has not become clear! Sending the client a précis of any conversation also helps to cement the bond and creates a favourable impression. This is even more the case when fact finding later. For the client there are few things worse at work than to spend time explaining the basics to an outsider who he or she never sees or hears from again!

Deciding Which Projects to Take On

Most assignments carried out by in-house consultants are short-term, perhaps only a couple of conversations. It is clearly not worth spending a great deal of time deciding how to spend a little. Time must be budgeted even for simply responding to managers in the organization. It is usually impossible to tell where any contract might lead and therefore to estimate any benefit. Deciding where to work and which managers to contact directly becomes important with larger projects.

All trainers, however they work, are faced with the same problems and need to put into place similar mechanisms to help solve them. Wherever possible, training objectives should be gleaned from the organization's operational or business plans and aimed at making a direct contribution to achieving organizational objectives.

The training function itself should generate a plan of action with a list of prioritized objectives. The description of how objectives will be met should include reference to in-house consultancy where appropriate and details of other methods, such as a programme of courses, administrative support, etc.

Bid Decisions

For larger projects it is helpful to have a procedure when considering whether or not to take it on. A simple checklist, such as that shown in Figure 5.5 may help. This type of checklist can help you to ask the necessary questions at the beginning of the project and to avoid mistakes (and regrets) later.

REFLECTIVE QUESTION 5.2

What are the practical difficulties of charging for internal consultancy services?

Costing Services

In our experience few internal consultants charge other departments for their services. Where they do it is usually part of an organizational system of project based cost centres (such as in design firms) supported by detailed costings and accounting systems. Everyone charges everyone else for their time.

However, this practice of cross-charging does seem to be on the

Primary Considerations

The answer to the following questions needs to be 'yes' before starting.

	YES	NO
Objectives		
Do project objectives match organization's objectives?		
Resources		
Do I have the necessary skills?		
Timetable		
Can I fit this work in?		
Context		
Is this appropriate work for me?		
Does this clash with my department's objectives?		
Personal		
Will this enhance my own position?		

Secondary Considerations

If the answers to the following questions are 'no', more work is needed.
It should be possible to start the project with some problems outstanding.

	YES	NO
Objectives		
Have I clarified the objectives?		
Do I agree with them?		
Resources		
Are other resources required?		
Can I acquire these resources?		
Timetable		
Do I know how long it will take?		
Does it clash with other commitments?		
Context		
Will it attract more work?		
Do I want to attract such work?		
Personal		
Will I enjoy this?		

Figure 5.5 *Bid decision checklist*

increase, especially in the public sector. Compulsory competitive tendering for services and the separation of purchasing and providing functions in Local Authorities and the Health Service have both forced many services, including training, to examine their costs and develop fairly detailed charging systems.

Even where cross-charging is not required, a full understanding of the costs and benefits of how you spend your time is vital for evaluation of work and decisions on what to do next. For example, if an individual's time costs out at £200 per day, is it really worth spending half a day visiting a video review centre to view a film, or would it be cheaper to hire it for £120 and spend just half-an-hour looking it through in the office? It rather depends on whether you can earn the £120 during the rest of the morning!

The costs of your service

In general, internal consultants' costs consist of their salaries and on-costs (employers' taxes, pensions, etc), plus a contribution to the over-heads of their department and organization. Which costs are included is often a politically motivated decision depending largely on why any costing exercise is carried out and who needs to be convinced of the trainer's cost effectiveness.

A typical checklist of staffing costs is presented in Figure 5.6, which should enable you to start working out your cost per day.

Fee earning ratio

By no means all the time spent at work can reasonably be charged to individual projects. The following activities need to be carried out:

- Marketing and talking to future clients
- Personal development and training
- Product assessment
- External liaison
- Departmental administration and briefing sessions
- Discussions and advice to clients and colleagues
- Working for anyone who doesn't pay a fee
- Thinking and looking out of the window.

This 'non-fee earning' time still has to be paid for. It is either lumped together and charged to a central budget figure or is apportioned across the fee-earning time by increasing the charge per day above the cost per day worked out above.

$$\frac{\text{Cost}}{\text{Charge}} \times 100 \ = \ \text{\% of fee-earning time}$$

An individual's 'fee-earning ratio' is a valuable indicator of how his or her time is being spent. Trainers whose role is primarily to manage a group of others, obtain work through marketing, and administer a department may well set themselves a fee-earning target of 50 per cent. One whose job is primarily working on specific projects set up by others may be aiming for 80-85 per cent. Fee-earning ratios of 95-100 per cent are a warning that not enough time is being devoted to personal development or

Data Sheet for Your Own Department

No. of staff in training dept.____
No. of purely support staff.........____
% Employer's N.I. contribution.........____
% Employer's pension contribution.........____
Expenditure for financial year.......................____
No. of working days per year................................____
No. of training or preparation days per year (guess!).........____

OVERHEADS TO RECOVER

Support Staff	1	2	3
Name			
Salary x WTE*			
Geog. Allow.			
N.I. Cont.			
Pension Cont.			
Other 1			
Other 2			
Total			

EMPLOYMENT COSTS TO RECOVER

Professional Staff	1	2	3
Name			
Salary x WTE*			
Geog. Allow.			
N.I. Cont.			
Pension Cont.			
Other 1			
Other 2			
Total			

*Whole time equivalent

Figure 5.6 *Checklist of costs*

planning for the future. It can be thought of as the consultant's equivalent of overtrading, when current projects end there will be no more work to do because no time has been devoted to marketing. Improving the fee-earning ratio is a powerful motivator or target to set yourself or your staff. Finding out what it is at the moment is a valuable exercise in how your time is spent.

Keeping track of time spent

A personal timesheet is a valuable record of how time is being spent and can form the basis of reports (or invoices) of time spent on a project. A typical example is shown in Figure 5.7. It can be made small enough to fit into a diary or 'Filofax' type organizer, or worked up as a spreadsheet in a personal computer. At the end of each day, the number of hours spent on each aspect of work is recorded and totalled. At the end of each month, or week if preferred, the total for each project can be totalled. Some nasty shocks can be had when the figures show neglect of one project, or the amount of time being consumed by another. Dividing work up in this way helps with personal organization and time planning. If the project divisions match your filing system you are halfway to getting organized.

Writing Proposals

Having arrived at a joint understanding of the client's situation and determined a suitable approach, it is important to define how the consultant will assist the client and what the client must do. It should also build the level of trust and confidence in the consultant by giving a professional and logical appearance. Above all, any proposal of services should address the client's problems and speak his or her language. An effective structure for proposals is as follows:

- Terms of reference from client.
- Consultant's comments on terms of reference.
- Specifications or description of services with who does what.
- Details of evaluation and monitoring systems.
- Benefits and costs to client.
- CVs of staff involved.
- Department's experience of similar work.

Terms of reference and consultant's comments

These define the scope of the proposal and often describe how the objectives for the project came to be established. Occasionally the client's terms of reference may be considered inappropriate or ambiguous, in

	1	2	3	4	5	6	7	8	9	10	11	12	13	14	15	16	17	18	19	20	21	22	23	24	25	26	27	28	29	30	31	SUBJECT	TIME	FILE
																																Career counselling		3.01
																																Appraisal Trg		19.01
																																Tele sales		
																																Supervisor course		22.01
																																Learning centre		23.00
																																Needs analysis		23.01
																																Design		23.02
																																Specifications		23.03
																																Admin & Prep		
																																Self Development		
																																Leave		
																																Grand Total		

Figure 5.7 *A personal timesheet*

which case the consultant will need to provide clarification or criticism.

Specifications or description of services

This section of a proposal varies according to the nature of the work to be undertaken. For investigations such as training needs analysis, it will be a description of the methodology and timetable of work. Specific outcomes will be impossible to specify but how the results will be presented and when, certainly can. Design work, such as writing courses or learning materials, needs very careful consideration. In general the specific learning objectives to be achieved by the target audience will be specified, together with a description of the delivery method (text, video, presented course, etc). The design methodology will be described, together with deadlines and budget restraints.

Proposals to organize and present training events or programmes can be more specific, giving course lists, target audience, frequency, duration, etc.

One of the benefits of working as an internal consultant is that the trainer need not fear giving too much away in the proposal for no payment. External consultants often put a great deal of time and expertise into preparing proposals which often provide the prospective client with enough information, presented very professionally, to persuade colleagues to do the job internally. The knack with proposals to prospective clients outside one's own organization is to give enough information to convince the client that the writer can do a good job, without doing it all.

Details of evaluation and monitoring systems

This section of the proposal will be more or less elaborate, depending on the size of the project. It should be included even in the shortest piece of work to reassure the client and to gain his or her commitment to gathering the necessary data, or even attending relevant reviews if applicable.

Benefits and costs to client

The structure and content of this section will depend strongly on the budgetary systems in place in the consultant's organization. It is important here always to sell the benefits of carrying out the project in terms that are valuable to the client. This section should link very strongly to the terms of reference above.

Costs should be broken down to estimate:

1. Client's own and staff's time.
2. Consultant's own and staff's time.
3. Travel expenses and subsistence.

71

4. Accommodation costs.
5. Equipment costs.
6. Consumables costs .

Who (or which budget centre) is charged for what should be made very clear from the start.

CVs of staff involved

Short, relevant details of the staff involved, including yourself, are useful, again to build the confidence of the client. Well set up consultants retain extended CVs of themselves and their staff on word processor files. Relevant paragraphs are brought out and reworded into a suitable short biography for inclusion in the proposal. As new projects are undertaken by staff they are added to the CV.

Department's experience of similar work

Here again, it is possible to build client confidence by providing short summaries of previous successes. Proposal writing can be greatly simplified by having potted histories on file. These should be written as part of the final project evaluation since they form a useful focus to extract learning from work just done. Proposals need not be long documents. Even a one page summary memo, such as the example in Figure 5.8, benefits from containing all the elements.

Case Study

Two or three weeks later Liz was able to look back with some satisfaction on what she felt she had been able to achieve. She had started off being clear in her own mind that her first and primary task at this stage was to gain people's confidence and then gather just sufficient data to put a plan of action to Jim with some degree of credibility.

Her initial agreement with him was to talk to the supervisors about the management courses they had attended and then get their ideas on what could be applied to improve the immediate situation.

Obviously she set out to do this in the knowledge that Jim had already formed some preconceived ideas about the issues, such as the outside training not going far enough to equip his supervisors to be better at their jobs. Whatever she was able to draw out of the situation, be it a diagnosis as a prelude to a solution or a list of symptoms of what might be amiss, she would have to take into account his standpoint if she was to be able to bring about something new.

In the first week she prepared some simple questions which she used in the form of a semi-structured interview when she came to talk to the supervisors. However it didn't work out exactly as she had planned.

To start with she received short answers to some of the questions about the job situation and about the course. One of the supervisors said she was quite happy in the job, she didn't feel she had any training needs although she had enjoyed the course she had attended. Her main comment was: 'Well I think it is up to management to make the job go better and give us training if something new has to be done. I have been here 12 years and I think I am generally on top of things, not like some others who have been here only a little while. The course was nice as a change, and I think I deserved to be sent on it, but not much new came out. It was good to hear that what I had been doing for years was the same as they talked about, handling staff, getting the best out of time and money available, things like that.'

The other supervisors answered in a similar way with a few differences. One made a few oblique criticisms of his boss, leaning forward and lowering his voice.

The problem (or issue) seemed to be that the staff had quite a lot to say but it was about things that Liz thought she didn't want to know, as not being relevant. She kept asking herself while a person was speaking, 'Does this help me build up a picture of what is going on, challenge Jim's perception of things, move me towards a 'solution', or is all this unrelated?'

However, matters seemed to improve thereafter. Liz made a list of her conclusions:

1. Supervisors had a reasonably positive view of the course though they did not identify a great deal of application to themselves.
2. How accurately were their needs assessed before they were nominated to attend courses?
3. They were not negative about their jobs but had views about their responsibilities which suggested either an unclear situation or one that their manager might want to change.

4. Did job descriptions need rewriting?
5. How can supervisory staff be made or persuaded to accept responsibility?
6. Is there an attitude problem?

Although uncomfortable, Jim had listened with interest and had appeared to agree with her assessment of the situation in general terms. He added that he was not surprised that Liz had not been able to get more from the supervisors as they were not all that forthcoming with him. He found it more appropriate to let them get on with their jobs although he felt the management course ought to have made them come into his office with some new ideas and suggestions.

Liz had then gone away and looked at her notes again. She found that she had tried to record all sorts of odd bits of material and when she came to read it afterwards was not always able to remember why she had made the note. Then came the problem when she started to sift the report in order to get something typed. The temptation was to put in a point which with hindsight was not really significant but nevertheless it ought to go in to give a feeling of completeness.

Liz used the opportunity offered to sit in on a staff meeting at which Jim Broadhurst was present together with the supervisors and most of the other staff. A little later she talked to the supervisors again with Jim present. She wanted to try something out.

This time she tried to hold the issues she had clarified and agreed with Jim in her mind while listening hard to what was being discussed. Her questions and comments stayed with the points brought out by individuals rather than trying to steer the discussion to where she thought it should go. At the end she was able to summarize, going back to her original points while at the same time adding on and integrating new aspects which had emerged.

She had now agreed to spend an hour or two during the next week looking at office documentation, job descriptions and a few other related papers. Then she would identify the issues or problems in priority order with either some suggestions on what might be done and by whom or any other relevant recommendations.

Presentation Skills for
In-house Contract Presentations

We refer to our conversation with A. Manager: your department wishes to allow members of staff to practise their presentation skills in the context of presenting in-house tenders to a selection committee.

The principal aims are to 'break the ice' and identify areas of further training need.

At the end of the session participants should be able to:
1. structure their presentations;
2. stick to time;
3. prepare good visual aids;
4. deal with questions on detail and strategy from the panel;
5. identify areas of further work required.

Methods
The afternoon will be as participative as possible with short briefings by the trainer followed by practice and comment.

Section 1   An example of poor practice from trainer.
              A feedback sheet for criticism from audience.
              Example of better presentation answering criticisms.

Section 2   Making an impression.

Section 3   Preparation of a section of a contract document for presentation to a panel of trainers and experienced staff.
              Two groups of 3 participants present this to panel.
              Self-appraisal and feedback from panel and colleagues.

Section 4   Summary of way forward.

Evaluation
The effectiveness of the programme will be determined by our standard post-course question-naire

Venue and time
Rooms 2 and 3 Training Centre, 1.30 – 5pm 10 Sept.

Staff involved
The session will be run by A. Trainer who has 7 years experience in training presentations and has run our in-house presentation skills programme for the past 3 years. She will draw on our department's extensive library of materials and hand-outs for your staff.

Costs
By running the programme in this way costs will be kept to a minimum.

A typical quote from an external consultant would be about £500 for such a session. I am confident that our approach will compare with the best.

If this proposal meets your requirements we will be able to arrange a short meeting to finalize a detailed programme within 10 days.

Figure 5.8   *Sample proposal of training services*

▶ PROGRAMME OF ACTION ◀

Review of last chapter's action
At the end of the last chapter we asked you to consider the stages in transition from your current methods to a predominantly consultancy role and how these stages could be introduced.

In general we have found that trainers have adopted the role gradually by responding to new demands in an increasingly consultant-like style and then by re-examining current work to see if it too can be approached differently.

Action for this chapter
Carry out a personal SWOT analysis.

Calculate your cost per day, keep a time log and estimate your fee-earning ratio and calculate a suitable charge per day to recover all your costs.

Rewrite your CV as a series of self-contained events (emphasize successes) for reference.

Review the work of your department. Write one page summaries of successful projects, with a picture or diagram for interest if possible, in a standard format. Place on file for future proposals.

Review a coming project, or one recently started; write a short proposal following the structure described above.

Get working with someone you have been avoiding or prefer in general not to work with.

6 Skills and Techniques – Data Collection, Identifying Problems and Agreeing the Contract

▷   SUMMARY   ◁

In this chapter we move on to discuss the key issues and activities which arrive after the initial contract, which may have come about in various ways, has been made. Particularly important is the whole process of gathering data both to determine what the issues are and also to take the necessary action agreed. We draw attention here to the need to define the issues in order to clarify the objections on which the contract will be based.

Other matters of concern will be the nature of the assignment (is it a problem?) and of ownership and stake holding (who cares about the outcome?). Beyond this there will be managing the data to bring about agreement to the terms of the assignment including who does what and when. This will be essential to monitor a record progress.

After reading through this chapter and working through the suggested tasks and applications, you should be able to:

- decide data required and possible means of acquiring it
- collect and present data
- negotiate within a particular situation a consultancy contract
- improve your listening skills.

We have already looked at how a trainer can start to operate a consultancy style of delivery. As a reminder, we always need to ask ourselves questions about the context of a particular project and the consequences of undertaking it.

We now move a little further on to the key issues arising from the initial contact, whether a request, an invitation or the expression of interest. These must include the initial process of gathering data and working out not only where to find out, but the equally important matter of sorting out what is relevant from what is unlikely to be of value. Relevant data become information. There are important stages here concerning gathering data to identify issues which will lead to the formulation of objectives, and thence to some form of contract or agreement which will structure the assignment. Additionally, there is gathering data in order to implement what has been agreed in the contract. Whatever form of training action or operational activity is carried out some new data will be called for. Within these prime activities are issues of the nature of the assignment (is it a problem?) and of ownership and stake holding (who cares about the outcome?) Beyond this there will be managing the data and presenting it to bring about agreement to the assignment, including who does what and when. This will be essential both to monitor and record progress as well as to assess success and validate outcomes.

What Sort of Data

REFLECTIVE QUESTION 6.1

What sort of data are you likely to need and how will you get them?

Perhaps you noticed something about the categories of data you decided upon in response to this question. Some of the items are needed in a particular sequence, some are dependent on the answers to earlier questions. Some of your questions may be concerned with deciding what the problem is and whether what has been outlined is a 'problem' or an 'issue'. Other questions may already be assuming there is a problem, assuming a need has been established and may be suggesting a solution, possibly one that is already available 'on the shelf'.

What seems to emerge here is that when we think randomly of the information we require, the questions are taken for granted. The questions may be subjectively skating round the whole issue, rather than getting to the heart of things. There may be no logic to the information we are seeking, no structure to the body of material we need. Perhaps what we need is a conscious pattern of questioning linked to a pre-determined model of a check list to ensure the trainer is more likely to get the right data in the right order. Let us take an example:

At a recent heads of department meeting attended by your manager a training issue (on the face of it) is raised by the Communications – Internal Services Manager. Your manager asks you to contact the individual concerned, who has some sort of 'trouble with understanding and responding to requests for up-to-date printouts' and 'statistical returns not always produced on time and in the way people can use for purposes appropriate to their own departments'. A meeting is arranged between you, as the in-house trainer, and the appropriate manager. There may be a consultancy assignment needed or requested.

The difficulty with this type of request is that the problem presenting may not, in truth, be the real problem in the workplace. It may be an expression of dislike or a symptom of some deeper disorder. The initial questions have to clarify the nature of the circumstances prompting the project before progress can be made.

Is it a Problem?

What we are trying to establish is a focus from which we can draw out objectives for the project as a whole. If we have been drawn in to something which has been perceived as a 'problem' does this mean something that has gone wrong, the so-called 'deviation from standard', or does it merely mean an issue which is not perceived negatively but positively as a challenge? That is why it is more useful to ask: 'What is the issue here and is there more than one?'

Identify the Issue

So our first step is: identify the issue. Data collected then must be sifted to provide information and only that which helps this identification.

This is not always going to be that simple. The issue itself is a reflection of how the originating manager sees it, a matter of personal perceptions. Don't rely on a rising rate of labour turnover, new procedures, a change in operations, a tide of complaints, to suggest a training or change intervention on the basis that 'the facts speak for themselves'. Perception will take us back to the personality and experience of the individual and any personal axes to grind which may be around. It can be useful to think about this when you start to collect data by asking the originator about the issue.

Gathering the Data

It will be helpful to start with the project file introduced in Chapter 5. It doesn't take long in our experience to accumulate assorted job descriptions, policy statements, notes from interviews, memos, with extra material. Papers are best kept in strict date order. Notes in the margin which indicate where evidence cross-refers, overlaps or incorporates other material (or contradicts it), will help to plan, monitor and control the whole process. If the structure of the final report is decided early in the project the file can be structured to match, which will greatly facilitate its preparation and the drawing of conclusions. With the right sort of organization the file can be a basis of a formal presentation if required, a quick progress round-up face-to-face with a manager, or a reference source for future work of a like kind.

You may need diary entries, lists of dates for seeing people, notes of telephone calls to make. These are planning and action triggers, helping you to make use of your time and determine what has to be done, as well as providing a stimulus for just getting on and doing it. We all need these tools to maintain progress and integrate a whole range of seemingly unrelated tasks and chores.

Whom should you see for data? The originator of the issue has already been mentioned. Others will be those who are influenced by or are part of the issue. The staff and colleagues, senior and peer of the originator; customers, clients and consumers of various kinds. All may have a different outlook and a different perception. Here you have the double reference value serving to underline the somewhat subjective accuracy which is found when one person's views are taken as gospel. A careful comparison of the mounting pile of evidence should help at both stages of data collection, identifying the issue and then later on producing a response, answer or solution.

It is not only people – stake holders with an interest or concern in the issue and any change which takes place affecting that issue – who represent a source of data. There will be published sources, there will be files, records, reports. We will often find one source will lead to another and each may offer something to clarify the picture.

Whether we are talking to managers, sitting in on staff meetings or interviewing customers we will be displaying and practising essential consultancy skills – asking questions, clarifying responses, making summaries and agreeing them, listening, prompting and probing. We will use a whole battery of techniques to apply these skills.

Check and Clarify

So we move to our second stage: check and clarify. We have already mentioned data gathering to identify the issue as well as moving beyond the contract stage. It will be important not to spend too much time gathering data beyond what is required for us to gain agreement to carry on. This is certainly true of external consultants, who have to balance credibility against excessive consumption of unpaid time and labour. In the same way as an internal consultant, the more conventional trainer must ensure that agreement is reached as to what the issue is and thence from objectives associated with a successful outcome, plus the structure of the route – time, money, resources, methods – to reach that outcome.

Agree the Issue with the Client

All we have done so far is a preliminary survey. We are now in a position to say something like this: 'You asked me to look at ... and these are my preliminary conclusions ... I think the situation is ... would you agree?' It is important to emphasize this third stage: agree the issue with the client. Let us assume this is accepted at least in principle. We now have a degree of issue ownership, a feeling of responsibility, a modicum of commitment and a potential for support. These will be important to encourage acceptance of responsibility to implement change and to develop self-reliance at the time when we have to discontinue our involvement.

There may be some negotiation, although fundamental disagreement should not arise if we have been clarifying and checking carefully and conscientiously as we were going along, albeit limited by the shortage of time.

Next, let us move from issue to objective. Successful outcome depends on how the issue has been identified. It may be removal of the 'deviation from standard'. It may be opportunity as the flip side of problem. It may be some new state of affairs, or a departmental objective where the issue is a blockage or barrier to the achievement of that objective. Here the client may have his or her own ideas and there will be the need to find some common ground. Failure to do this could lead you to taking on something you are not happy with. The failure to agree to mutual satisfaction will be compounded at all subsequent stages of the assignment.

Agree Objective or Outcome Indicating Success.

This is the fourth stage of the process. Thinking about this will suggest to you all sorts of success criteria which will govern the contract you are accepting and engaging in. For example, consider:

- What you set out *to achieve?*
- In what *space of time?*
- In terms of how much *personal involvement?*
- Possibly, at what *cost?*
- With what *resources and help* from the client?
- Through what means of *monitoring, control review* and *reporting?*

For brevity these are often linked to aspects of quantity, quality, cost and time or more simply just as outcomes and methods, which would include a whole range of inputs.

Agree Inputs, Limitations and Constraints

The term 'contract' has been used in some places interspersed with 'agreement'; it may be formal or it may be informally nominal.

REFLECTIVE QUESTION 6.2

How acceptable would one of your potential clients find a contract and in what form?

It will be worth asking around to compare your answer with the views of your potential clients.

The outline contract given above can form a useful checklist of items to be agreed with the client and to help structure early conversations.

Useful Listening Behaviours

The skills and techniques of data gathering, as already indicated, apply to all stages of a consultancy assignment, including interchanges leading up to a negotiated contract. We describe here some of the behaviours which will help underpin some of these skills and activities.

Clarifying

The simplest form of intervention from the listener is to seek clarification of something he has not understood.

In order to indicate to the speaker that you do not seek him to enlarge on the point, but merely to explain it, questions of clarification are best framed fairly specifically and tend to start with 'who', 'what', 'where' or 'when'. Questions starting with 'why' are usually far more complex and challenging to the speaker, taking them back into their general values, beliefs and motivations rather than to the more specific explanation required. 'Why' questions are discussed further under 'Probing' below.

Reflecting back data

Restating back a client's key words as they are spoken will usually cause them to expand on that idea or explain in more detail what is in their mind. Typically, the listener will interject the client's word into the conversation with a questioning inflection, eg:

CLIENT: 'Of course the profit margins are too tight ...'
CONSULTANT: 'Profit margins?'
CLIENT: 'Yes. At only 27 per cent we can't ...'

Repeating the term 'profit margins' forces the client to expand on it. To avoid sounding parrot-like the listener can use slightly different interjections such as:

'You mentioned profit margins ...' or
'Tell me more about profit margins ...' or
'I am interested in profit margins ...'

Reflecting back a term such as 'profit margins' will tend to provide mostly factual data. In the example above the listener could have chosen to reflect back the term '... too tight'. This would generally bring out information on the speaker's values or beliefs about the situation;

CLIENT: 'Of course the profit margins are too tight ...'
CONSULTANT: 'Too tight?'
CLIENT: 'Yes, the way I am being pegged back I don't think we will survive beyond the summer ...'

Reflecting back is clearly not a neutral activity and the listener needs to use a nice sense of touch and timing to help the client explain his situation.

Picking up on particular aspects more than others can create a feeling in the client of being criticized or manipulated, which causes resentment, mistrust and closing up.

Paraphrasing

Another behaviour available to the listener is to paraphrase and say back to the speaker what has just been said. This allows the listener to check his understanding and to demonstrate that understanding to the speaker.

This is a valuable way of structuring the discussion into manageable 'chunks' and allows time for the listener to internalise what has been said.

The listener should only use this method when confident that the speaker has been understood. The client can be upset if the paraphrasing is inaccurate. The consultant may be accused of trying to 'put words into the client's mouth'.

Typically the listener would introduce such an intervention with words like:

'Can I just go through that again, you say that ...' or
'So you are saying that ...' or (more jargon ridden)
'Can I run that past you again ...'

Summarizing

If paraphrasing produces 'chunks', summarizing divides the discussion into 'sections'.

Everyone is aware of the need to summarize what has been said at the end of a discussion. Fewer people seem to realize its value at key points during one. Summarizing where you have been and what ground has been covered is an ideal opportunity to take brief, agreed notes and to decide where to go next. Both participants feel that useful progress is being made and further benefits can be obtained by carrying on.

Summarizing serves to reinforce joint understanding and to build confidence in the value of the process, adding energy to the conversation.

Probing

Probing is a process of asking questions to find out more information than has been given so far. It is a controlling activity and is generally led by the consultant's value system and need to feel confident and well informed. It also helps a client to examine his or her own understanding of the position.

Probing questions asked before sufficient trust or understanding has developed can be interpreted by the client as aggressive, nosey or threatening behaviour. If this happens the client either becomes less likely to explain or clams up completely. Again good judgement is needed in its use.

The 'Why?' question

We mentioned above under 'clarification' the fundamental difference between questions beginning with 'why' and those beginning with 'who', 'what', 'when', 'which' and 'where'. Fig. 6.1 illustrates the nature of this difference.

'Why' questions take the discussion back towards the general and backwards in time. Each 'why/because' question and answer leads towards underlying strategy rather than tactics, towards the core values and beliefs of the client. Such techniques are valuable when trying to get to the root of business decisions and resolving in-built conflicts. They are

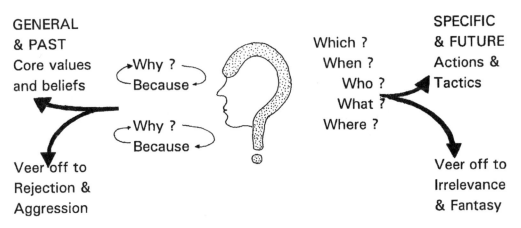

Figure 6.1 *The 'Why' Question*

also very challenging to individuals who must ultimately reveal personal views and motivations which they may not consider to be in the public domain.

Alternatively they may show that the client is unaware of the reasons behind his or her actions or that the reasons conflict with company or 'accepted' wisdom. The result of such problems will be familiar to anyone who has had dealings with three year old children during their 'Why, Daddy?' phase. Fairly soon the parent becomes confused or irritated with the child and may end up rejecting the questioning ('... go away and play'), or by becoming aggressive, ('Because I say so!'). Similar reactions await consultants who press such questioning too far, too fast or too early on in their relationships with clients.

'What', 'which', etc questions take the discussion into ever greater detail of tactics and action or greater detail of the current position.

What if
'Why' questions tend to look back to the past and to causes. 'What if' questions, on the other hand, look to the future and to consequences. They are useful for testing the robustness of plans and decisions. Simple questions can develop into sophisticated choice diagrams to explore various possible future scenarios for contingency planning. Alternatively they can degenerate into time-wasting flights of fancy.

Two useful questions
Two useful questions which help managers to describe their situations in specific terms are:

- What's not happening that should be?
- What's happening that shouldn't?

These produce information on behaviours and outcomes, both of which are central to any training or change project.

When sifting through the material on file we remind ourselves of some conceptual pitfalls. Opinions sometimes come to us as facts. We may need to probe, check and agree whether what is put forward is hearsay, personal interpretation or objective data capable of being separately and independently substantiated. Another thought is that it is much easier for people to make judgements than to make judgements backed up by reasons. Even if the judgement is necessarily a personal one it is helpful to see what evidence has led to that judgement. Similarly, wide, sweeping generalized statements put forward as accurate pictures of a particular situation are common enough contributions.

An Implementation Schedule

Your contract may be a bit general: you will develop some training by the end of three weeks from today; you will rewrite some job descriptions and update a tailored piece of training to fit by the 30th. Alternatively you may want to agree some stages of implementation – further data gathering, the submission of preliminary proposals, consultation on these, Phase I implementation – against set dates. It will probably depend on the size of the project, how many variables and people are involved, degrees of complexity and ambiguity in the situation and so on. A key principle in implementing any change process is carrying people with you, involvement, gaining agreement and thereby commitment. This means feedback and review. The longer you go on without reporting back, the more likelihood there will be of getting out of touch with the client. You will continually be reforging the link and rebuilding the relationship. It is always worth considering your review mechanism, that is, how you and your client will ensure satisfactory progress is being made.

REFLECTIVE QUESTION 6.3

What review methods can you think of? Do they vary with the size and duration of the project? Are they a hammer to crack a nut?

Bearing in mind the tremendous variation of tasks, projects and assignments the consultant trainer can come across you might usefully list some possibilities you can think of. One-to-one meetings between trainer and client are likely to be the most appropriate; you might also consider written reports, summaries and analyses of results.

Case Study

At last a clearer picture seemed to have emerged. Having checked her material and having sorted her notes into a better order, throwing away odd papers as necessary, Liz was able to conclude:

1. All the supervisors had job descriptions which contained vague items and others out of date or not entirely acceptable. The reason seemed to be that they had been compiled some time in the past and had been extracted from similar documents from Broadhurst's previous job.
2. The supervisors seemed not to have any common understanding about their objectives.
3. There appeared to be little in the way of explicit performance standards. Although an informal appraisal scheme operated it appeared to be run on very subjective lines largely on a 'telling' basis.
4. The supervisors morale was not really low. Rather they seemed to be complacent about their work and content to accept a strong and perhaps even 'dictatorial' lead from above.
5. There seemed to be a problem about some of the work concerning other departments. Some of the Appeals administration was carried out in the department, which caused some discontent and bad feeling between the supervisors and their colleagues at the same level elsewhere. There were also other areas like this – some statistical analysis work, accounts processing and some copy typing – all of which seemed to be a hangover from some agreement made in the past. Probably at the time it was intended to be a temporary arrangement.
6. Some obvious skill and knowledge deficiencies had

shown up. These included what might be termed leadership style' (the supervisors' way of relating to the staff in their sections was substantially the same as the way that Jim Broadhurst related to and communicated with them). Other items were updating on some of the new data processing systems, public relations, and counselling techniques.

In Jim Broadhurst's office Liz went over this ground trying to gain agreement and to consolidate the position step by step. Mindful of the principles she had agreed with him earlier, she was determined to involve him in order to carry everything forward on a joint action basis.

The problem was that although he agreed that some of the items identified by her were accurate, he did not see them as a priority for action, or even that anything needed to be done at all. In summary:

Job descriptions
'I've been meaning to do something about this one, leave it with me.'

Objectives
'I don't wonder. We're all confused. I expected more to come out of the new line from the Board especially with all the work going on about 'future looks' and on the mission statement. I shall push this one hard at the HOD's meeting next month. I'm glad you brought it up, it's been at the back of my mind for some time.'

Attitudes
'This doesn't really worry me. What it comes to is that we all have a job to do. They have theirs and I have mine.'

Allocation of work
'Well … yes I suppose if you put it that way, but these people's managers don't come to me with complaints and I can't be around to chase up every little thing myself. It seems to work reasonably well and my colleagues do things for me as well. Can we agree to leave that one for a bit and I'll have a think about it?'

Skills and knowledge deficiencies
'Yes this is the sort of thing I had in mind when I asked you to come and spend a bit of time having a look round and talking

to my staff. Could you do some training here for us? ... Sort of carrying on from the management course the supervisors attended and also something for the rest of the staff as well.'
In the end a two-part plan was agreed.

LIZ: To run a short in-house programme for the three supervisors aimed at meeting the skills and knowledge shortfalls.
JIM: To sort out and clarify the job descriptions in time to feed into the training of the supervisors.

Liz was then able to secure Jim's agreement to a follow-up training session for the section staff carried out by the supervisors as part of an in-house action plan and also that he would get involved himself as part of a forum on the way ahead, priorities, the influence of new policies on how he saw the department's work changing. She sensed that maybe she was bullying him but he did agree.

▶ PROGRAMME OF ACTION ◀

Review of last chapter's action
In Chapter 5 we asked you to carry out a SWOT analysis. We hope that this has provided a clearer understanding of your own situation and a possible way forward as an internal consultant. There were a number of tasks designed to help you to write costed proposals.

Action for this chapter
Draft a specimen 'contract' as a checklist to ensure key points are clarified and then agreed.

If you have been able to try out your consultancy role you will already have some actual or potential assignments on your books. Here is an opportunity to test out the simple stages of identifying, clarifying and agreeing issues, setting and agreeing measurable objectives, in order to negotiate contracts as outlined in this chapter. At the same time try to see these processes in relation to the general approach given in Chapter 3 – gaining entry and agreement, research, implementation and disengagement. Try to analyse in hindsight a project you have completed and try to recognize each of the stages.

Obtain feedback from colleagues and friends about your listening style, using your own or a published questionnaire or checklist.

Practise especially each of the listening techniques described above in turn during your conversations, and make notes afterwards on how it went.

7 Skills and Techniques – Project Management, Learning Design and Implementing Change

▷.   SUMMARY   ◁

1. We concentrate on the kinds of review and project management systems suited to small projects. Small projects usually involve one or two consultant staff working with a manager in a specific department and these are most frequently carried out by in-house consultants. This is also the kind of work which is often thought too small or short to benefit from a formal approach to planning, monitoring and review. An example in action is the plan generated in Chapter 5 for introducing a consultancy style of working into a job.
2. We examine the in-house consultant's role in implementing changes in the workplace and some of the techniques which can be employed to help the process.
3. We describe techniques of project management and explain their relevance to the particular position of the in-house consultant.

After reading through this chapter and working through the various tasks you should be able to:

- plan a simple project and present ideas on a bar (Gantt) chart
- allocate resources and responsibilities to named individuals. Identify key players and their role in the project.
- set up and generate a review and monitoring system
- identify and respond to changes in working relationships with clients
- assist clients to implement and manage changes at work.

> ## REFLECTIVE QUESTION 7.1
>
> What problems would you envisage in running a consultancy project?

Project Control Mechanisms

However projects are managed, in detail or style, there are six principal elements to bear in mind :

1. Establishing clear objectives.
2. Planning for their achievement.
3. Determining standards to be achieved.
4. Monitoring performance.
5. Comparing with plans.
6. Correcting deviations or amending the plan.

Running throughout all these stages is the need for sound, effective communications with all the parties involved.

Establishing Clear Objectives

This area has been covered in detail in the two preceding chapters. We make no apologies for this emphasis. Clear objectives are the foundations of all work carried out in this mode. They ensure that you are doing 'the right thing'.

As an in-house consultant there are often more agendas (including your own and your department's) to consider than for the outsider and there may be more opportunity for conflicts of interest between the client and trainer. In our experience it is best to be open about such conflicts and seek to compromise.

A typical example regards the implementation of company policy on such things as equal opportunities which may go beyond the strict requirements of the law. The client manager may be half-hearted or actively disagree with aspects of policy which the trainer may feel obliged to support. Both parties need to be realistic and recognize the other's position. Simply ignoring these differences can lead to later conflicts.

It is often the shorter, less involved project which suffers from poorly defined objectives. Casual meetings in corridors or over lunch can be the start of interesting work but are usually too ill-defined to be worth putting in a lot of effort without stating clearly the objectives and agreeing them in writing.

Planning for their Achievement

Planning is a vital skill for success in any job. An in-house HRD consultant needs to be a skilled planner and should build up a repertoire of techniques which not only help in planning actions but which help others to understand the project and become involved.

Simple methods are therefore to be preferred where possible. Gantt (Bar) charts are an excellent method of communicating what is going on and who should be doing it.

Matrix methods such as responsibility charts, or communication charts are useful for the same reason. Critical path techniques (or 'PERT') on the other hand, are best saved for detailed planning and decision making on resource utilization for larger projects.

We do not intend to go into the detail of these methods, but interested readers are referred to the bibliography. Instead we shall use the action list developed in Chapter 5 and other simple examples to illustrate each technique in use.

Computer assistance

As personal computers become increasingly used a number of software programs are available to help plan and monitor the progress of projects. For major projects these are a godsend, enabling rapid establishment of the critical path, amounts of leeway on start and finish times ('float'), last start time, etc, and rapid updates following changes. For small projects they can become a real chore, taking up far more time than simple plotting on to graph paper or actually using the large dry-wipe board on your wall!

However, if you like computers, they are fun to use and usually produce excellent plans or diagrams to share with clients. Such plans help communications and help present a very professional image which increases the client's confidence in you and your methods.

The choice is largely up to the individual based on personal preference and level of use and support for such systems within the organization.

Figure 7.1 shows a typical bar chart showing the duration of each phase of the action plan. It also separates the work of the training assistant working in the office from that of the trainer acting as consultant.

Diagrams of this macro level are really of use in deciding strategy and helping the people involved to obtain a feel for what is going to happen. Far more detailed plans split down to individual responsibilities are required for adequate communication and control.

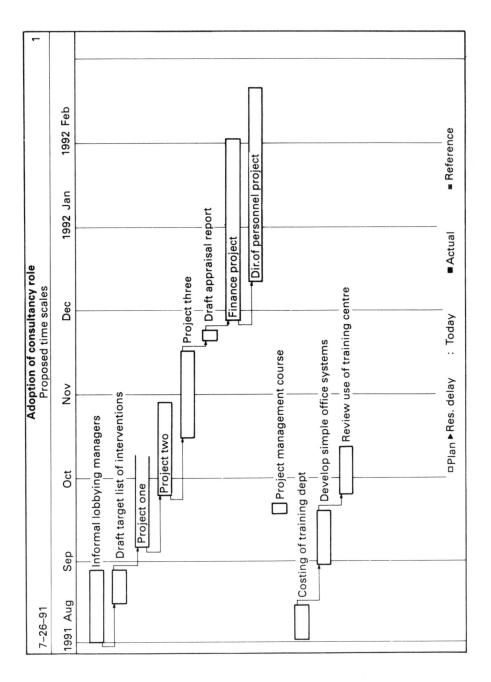

Figure 7.1 *Action plan bar chart*

Responsibility matrix

Simple tools work best. The responsibility matrix is a table of jobs to be done and people who are likely to be involved. Figure 7.2 gives an example where the contents of the boxes are a code describing who is responsible for something, who is doing it and who is expected to assist. Lots of additional entries can be used such as start and finish dates, and estimated staff time (especially if people are changing).

R – Responsible for D – Doing A – Assisting	Briefing staff on tele-sales ideas	Arranging Venue	Follow up interiews to identify training	Organising training as necessary
DAVID			R	R
HILARY			D	D
IAN	R D			
SUE	A	R D	A	

Figure 7.2 *Responsibility matrix*

Photocopying the document and circulating it to everyone named on the list is a powerful method of ensuring that people are clear about who does what. It also generates lots of feedback on design of the project and allocation of resources.

The communication matrix

More problems and arguments seem to be caused in projects due to oversights in communication than for any other reason. One advantage the in-house consultant has is a good knowledge of the organization's structure and the people in post. Such familiarity should not be squandered by assuming that colleagues, friends even, will get to know what is happening by osmosis. It is very important to think out who needs to know what and when. This will help determine the most appropriate mechanism for communication activity.

Figure 7.3 shows a typical matrix of people and information. Here two keys are used, one for the status and another for the method. Communication must be two-way, some key players must be consulted or have their permission sought before progress can be made, others need only be kept informed of what is happening.

This diagram is useful to share with the client to help ensure you haven't missed any key players or too many of the others. Bitter experience shows that there always seems to be someone who gets overlooked.

	Content of new job description	Date of briefing	Identification of training need interviews (purpose)	Identification of training need interviews (dates)
Sales staff	C / G	I / M	I / G	I/M
Sue	C / F	I / M	C / F	P / M
Ian	Source	I / M	C / F	I / M
Hilary	I / M	I / M	Source	Source

Key   Status of communication
I = For information, P = Permission required, C = Commitment required
   Method of communication
F = face to face, G = group briefing, M = Memo

Figure 7.3 *Communication matrix*
Individuals or groups are identified who must be involved in the communication exercise.
In this version both the method of communication and the desired outcome are stated.

The diagram can also be used as a basis for monitoring the communication activity and effectiveness during the project.

Determining Standards to be Achieved

While this is frequently done during the setting of objectives it is only after the planning and allocation of resources has occurred that timetables and standards can be agreed, as they are usually resource dependent.

Deadlines

The simplest and most frequently defined standards are deadlines. They are conveniently plotted on charts and recorded in diaries. They are also simple and unambiguous to monitor. Deadlines also give strong messages about the quality of work to be expected. If a report is asked for within one or two days, rather than as many weeks, it will be assumed that a short overview, not a detailed account, is requested. These are dangerous assumptions in general. If you are an in-house consultant you have an advantage over an external person in these matters since you are aware of the culture of the organization. You will be better able to judge what is required without needing to spend so much time defining parameters and standards. The more people work together the better is this understanding.

Costs

Setting a limit to expenditure for the project as a whole and its various components is a critical exercise. It is important to identify those aspects where costs cannot be closely predicted such as development time for new training products, investigation into problems, or building work. These need the most rigid definition and closest control. Clearly items of small cost (eg paper clips) or predictable cost (a tightly specified piece of equipment) need less control.

Quantity

Most of us can count. Quantities of things are attractive types of control standard as they are easy to measure. The knack is to make the important things measurable, not to make the measurable things important.

Typical counts are filled places in training events, the percentage of staff interviewed about needs analysis, or the number of questionnaires returned.

Quality Measures and Quality Assurance

Some of our colleagues (certainly not *us!*) have a guarded, slightly defensive view regarding quality measures in training and development activity. All agree that they are 'a good thing' but many balk at the prospect of keeping highly detailed records, designing a plethora of forms for a complex quality assurance scheme or spending valuable time which could be better spent 'doing the work'.

These views seem to have arisen as a result of a desire to produce a complete and unambiguous system of evaluation and assurance or to comply with seemingly complex, and not always relevant, national or international quality assurance standards (such as BS 5750 or ISO 9020). It is a prime example of 'Perfection being the enemy of the good'. Since perfection is seen as an impossible goal, no attempt at formal quality assurance is made.

In our experience the simplest of quality assurance systems can provide excellent results both in terms of improved work and personal confidence. As a trainer, whether acting in a consultancy mode or not it is important to have adequate and robust procedures, adequate expertise and resources and a method of monitoring that both are correctly and consistently applied. This is the basis of any good QA system.

Adequate procedures should exist for: receiving, filing and distributing correspondence (letters, fax, telex, etc), communications (telephone conversations, meeting records, principal contacts), applications to attend training.

Adequate advanced planning and review methods
The methods of working should be planned and agreed in advance with the client. Adequate planning is an integral part of quality assurance.

Clear learning objectives
Learning objectives, lessons, plans and evaluation systems should be written for all training events and maintained on file.

Suitably qualified and experienced staff
Records of training activity and experience should be kept on file to demonstrate suitability to clients.

A fee-earning ratio low enough to allow trainers to stay up to date or a target for time spent on subject updating (eg 20 per cent of time) is a valuable quality indicator.

Adequate cover in case of sickness or departure.

A suitable project file
Many studies generate lots of paper. Keeping organized helps the process enormously. A good filing system enables the user to tell the destination of anything that comes across his or her desk and where to find it again. A well kept file also tells the story of how a project has developed and why. How can this blissful position be achieved?

One effective system is to allocate one numbered file to each project and subdivide it according to the project plan. As an example, consider the refurbishment of a computer training centre. Since it is our first project we shall call it 01. The component parts of the project might be :

01.1   Project initiation and contact list.
01.2   Project planning and quality assurance.
01.3   Building and redecoration work.
01.4   Commissioning hardware and software.
01.5   Purchasing furniture.
01.6   Training programmes to be offered.
01.7   Marketing of facility.

Dividing the project file in this way enables each section to tell a sensible story and makes retrieval more straightforward. In addition, relevant parts can be held by different people if the jobs have been split among a team. Each section can be further subdivided if the size and the project merits it, eg:

01.3.1 Services (electricity, telecoms, etc).
01.3.2 Furniture and fixtures.
01.3.3 Painting and decorating.

Correspondence

If possible store correspondence separately from supporting documentation and notes. Many projects attract booklets, brochures, research documents, etc which are valuable source material but interrupt the usefulness of a correspondence file which should be like a recorded conversation. This is very useful when trying to clear up misunderstanding or clarifying decisions. These situations are often disagreements about 'who is right', so being able to find the relevant memo gives a good impression and is good for one's self-confidence. Folders equipped with built in paper fasteners and a separate pocket for booklets, etc, are a worthwhile investment, more than repaying their cost in saved time and aggravation.

A useful rule and habit is to write the destination file number on every piece of paper used. Not knowing the number to write is a sure sign of a poorly structured project.

This level of subdivision may equate to convenient budget centres against which to monitor the scheme. Equally it may be useful to record staff time input against each subsection. This helps ensure clients are not being overlooked and can assist future estimates of work time should similar projects be carried out. The file numbers can be used in association with the timesheet in Figure 5.7 (page 70).

Monitoring Performance

Any good system of project control should:

1. Concentrate on the critical aspects of the project.
2. Detect deviations from plan as early as possible.

In addition they should operate continuously, be flexible, be themselves under constant review and be clear and simple to operate.

Concentrate on the critical aspects of the project

These should be identified at the beginning of the project with the client. The traditional 'critical path' highlights only those activities which are critical to the duration of the project. Other elements may be critical due to the high reliance of other activities on their success, eg the quality of a learning design, their high public profile, such as a launch ceremony, or the personal preferences of clients or other key players.

Detect deviations from plan as early as possible

All important parts of the project should have measurable features identified before their final deadline. This enables action to be taken before the products are actually late.

For example, a programme design might be needed by 30 September. It is obviously of little use waiting until 1 October to see if it is on time. Design work is often difficult to plan and always takes longer than imagined. A typical plan might be as shown in Figure 7.4:

complete	%
Initial discussions	10
Learning objectives identified	15
Outline plan agreed	20
Individual session plans drafted	40
Individual session plans finalized	60
Training materials specified	75
Materials produced or purchased	85
Pilot run	90
Minor redrafts	95
Project completion	100%

Figure 7.4 *Time allocation in programme planning*

In our experience designing the overall programme is achieved early in the design but gives a deceptive sense of progress made. (In truth many trainers have reached this stage even before determining the learning objectives!) It is important to bear in mind that a great deal of time-consuming detailed work has to be done after this stage.

A useful measure of progress is the first drafting of session plans. Since the work required to get to this stage is about 40 per cent of the total design time it should be done within the first 40 per cent of time allowed for the overall project if that is to be delivered on time. All the critical aspects of the programme need to be divided up along these lines and so-called 'milestones' or 'deliverables' identified.

Comparing with plans
Tightly controlled projects usually have regular progress reports built into them. Such reports should be short to read, quick to write and link directly to the project plan. If possible a proforma outline of their contents should be agreed with the client. Reports should concentrate on exceptions and deviations from plans and proposals to rectify matters.

If there are no deviations from plans and things are going well, cancel the review and treat yourself and the project team to tea and cakes and warn them against complacency!

Controlling Committees

The progress of a project may be overseen by a committee of some type. This often happens when the project is part of a larger programme or where it is sufficiently wide-ranging to take it beyond the remit of an individual manager. If well managed, this can be a valuable method. It provides the trainer with access to all the interested parties in a convenient manner, can resolve differences of opinion and approach and can harness considerable resource and influence.

All too often such committees suffer from a lack of direction or, even worse, deep-seated differences in opinion about which direction to follow. Being at the receiving end of such guidance is extremely difficult and potentially damaging for the reputation of the consultant who may become the organizational scapegoat for the committee's failings.

Project Champion

To ensure a single vision of the way forward the consultant should try to identify, formally if possible, a project champion' at a higher level than the members of the committee. The champion's role is to provide a single vision to protect the workings of the committee from the demands of the rest of the organization and to provide an arbiter in disagreements.

The other important step is to facilitate the definition of project objectives with the committee as a whole. This is frequently a lengthy process but can be made more straightforward by appropriate lobbying of individual members before any meeting.

Making it easy for the whole group to arrive at a consensus over objectives increases the sense of ownership and encourages differences to emerge at an early stage.

Ill-formed Groups

Some committees become composed of people who simply have the time available or don't like to leave things to others. These are dangerous groups to work with since they may gain their satisfaction by exercising blocking powers (the 'I really showed them' type) or are unable to allow consultants any freedom to act (the 'who do they think they are?' type). Often committees become dominated by staff managers from Personnel, Finance or professional advisers rather than the line managers who have to live with the results. Without the relevant line managers the results of any work may lack line credibility and will certainly lack any appropriate ownership. In either instance the project is handicapped and is less likely to be effective in the workplace.

If line managers are absent from the committee and cannot be encouraged to join, extra time and attention must be paid to them during the work. The line managers shall be treated as the clients and the committee as the 'police force'. This can be helped by defining the committee's role, in its terms of reference, as a monitoring body of process and timetable rather than as an arbiter of the outcome.

We have probably all experienced examples of training programmes especially on policy matters such as health and safety or equal opportunities, which have been designed by Training- or Personnel-dominated groups and which have been largely ignored, or even sabotaged, by line managers who have not been truly involved in their formulation or convinced of their worth.

It is almost impossible to spend too much time consulting and trying to convince client managers and their staff.

Obstructive Groups

The final type of group we shall consider is the one set up to delay implementation or to give the impression of activity when there is no real intention to act. The classic example is the Government Inquiry or Royal Commission. Such groups are packed with large numbers of individuals all representing others, mostly with widely different values and views on what should happen. No decisions can be taken without reference back to individuals' constituencies, no statements can be made or decisions taken which are not hedged around with exclusions or exceptions. Reports take so long to produce that they are out of date and are so long that almost no one spends the time to read them.

Golden Rules for Project Control Groups

- Members should be there in their own right.
- Have the key line managers as members.
- Ensure the group reports to a project champion with a clear vision of purpose.
- Define terms of reference clearly: either a monitoring group or an executive one.
- Agree with the whole group the objectives and standards to be achieved.
- Keep the group informed of progress.
- Treat them with respect, however stupid they are.
- Keep the group as small as possible (4 or 5 is good).

Corrective deviations or amending the plan

When an individual's work is below standard or that person shows no enthusiasm for a project the consultant is faced with the fact that they don't report to him. Methods of persuasion and cajoling rely on his interpersonal skills, expert authority or conferred authority; either due to status or delegation from the client manager.

Internal consultants do not have as much conferred authority as external ones, they are more familiar and just another part of the organization. Their expertise has to be demonstrated rather than assumed. This throws them back on to their individual skills.

The internal consultant does, however, benefit from a greater knowledge of the organization and usually has a firmer relationship with the manager who needs to do the motivating.

Unrealistic expectations

Usually, however, performance problems are related to the individual's work situation. Projects which are part of the consultant's normal work load are usually extra and often unwelcome work for the staff in the department. If no allowance has been made for this the consultant may expect more than can reasonably be delivered. The second most common reason for under-achievement is that the individual can see no benefit in the work. This may be due to a failure to involve and convince them, or it may well be that there is nothing to benefit them. Indeed they may be under considerable threat.

Dealing with the human aspects of change is discussed below in the 'management of change'. As with all deviations from plan problems with individuals are best avoided by realistic and thorough planning. When difficulties are experienced, however, they should be described, without judgement, and discussed with the client, whose responsibility the project is. Do not usurp this responsibility, nor diminish the client's sense of it, by carrying on actions and corrections which are rightfully his or hers.

The Management of Change

There is a considerable literature on the management of change and the implications for trainers were touched on in Chapter 2. In our experience simple processes and techniques applied with determination will get the best results. We have already discussed the use of the 'SWOT' technique in Chapter 5. If you like mnemonics you might like the next stage – 'BEEF':

Build on the strengths.
Eliminate the weaknesses.
Enjoy the opportunities.
Face the threats.

This is a useful method of setting the agenda for change but doesn't always help decide how to act.

The Change Equation

Kurt Lewin (1947) noted that change will happen if :

$$\int D \times V \times K > \text{Resistance or cost.}$$

That is to say, change will happen if a function of the dissatisfaction with the current position (D) multiplied by the vision of the future (V) and knowledge of the first practical steps (K) is less than the resistance to change or the cost of bringing it about.

Dissatisfaction with the current position
People will be more likely to change if they are dissatisfied with the current position. Increasing current dissatisfaction was described in Chapter 5 under 'disconfirmation'. People need information on what is happening at the moment and the ill effects or likely ill effects in the future. Confronting people with the stark facts of shortcomings or poor quality is usually enough to produce the discontent necessary. Other techniques include 'confrontation' laboratories described by Bennis (1969), direct discussion with consumers and structured feedback from colleagues, perhaps using questionnaires.

Vision of the future
People will be more likely to change if they have a clear vision of how things could be in the future. Here again the project champion who is available to explain what the end state looks like is so valuable. An ideal or a Utopia is not usually credible. The vision needs to be explained, in person to the staff involved in terms they understand and value.

These explanations do not need to be Sermons from the Mount or Martin Luther King's promised land speech. They do need to be concise and well explained with rather more in the way of questioning than we recall Moses tolerating!

Knowledge of the first steps
It is not necessary for people to be able to see the entire path to the new condition as long as they know where to start and are confident of the general direction. At work the position is made clearer and less risky for

all, if a clear and coherent plan has been drawn. Individuals, especially those identified as possible obstructions, should have a recognized, specific role described for them and should be individually briefed and convinced before the plan is made generally available. This whole process requires planning and really good communications.

The nature of resistance to change

Successful organizations are stable and have built-in resistance to change. It is a vital part of any organization or individual; without it they could be diverted from their path by the smallest pressure or the slightest distraction. Bear this in mind when you next try to convince someone to alter their ways!

Change agents tend to work to reduce the resistance to change in general by altering organizational culture and systems (a very great challenge), or to reduce the resistance to specific changes which is often more productive in the short term. This latter strategy requires analysis of the resistances posed by individuals or specific situations.

Identifying the key players

Readiness mapping: Typical methods include domainal mapping or role set analysis (see Chapter 1) in which individuals or teams identify all the people with whom they communicate or interact in their jobs, noting features of the relationship.

Having plotted the key players it is often helpful to chart their individual positions with regard to the change now and what you would want them to be. Figure 7.5 shows an example.

	Pushing for Change	Neutral	Resisting the Change
ROBIN	X ←———— O		
CLARE		O X	
JANE		X ←———— O	

O = Current Position
X = Desired Position

Figure 7.5 *Readiness map*
Individuals are judged to be pushing for, neutral to or resisting a change.
A second jungement is made regarding the desired stance if the project is to be a success.

Robin is assessed as neutral to the change but is needed to be actively pushing. A lot of work and convincing must go on here.

Clare too is seen as neutral, which is, however, a satisfactory position so long as she doesn't move towards resistance.

Jane is seen as resisting change. She is not needed to push actively for the change but her resistance is harmful. Here too some work must be done to stop her resistance.

This method helps consultants to decide where to focus their energy and what types of persuasion are required.

Force field analysis: This is probably one of the most widely used and extremely useful methods. It is based on the idea that work situations represent a status quo where pushing and resisting forces are more or less equally balanced. Some of the forces – attitudes of key figures in the organization, local events, agreed policies, outside influences (and there are many more) – may be working towards a certain situation or outcome. Others will be working against that same situation or outcome. Force field analysis is a way of mapping these forces in order to understand the dynamic nature of what is going on.

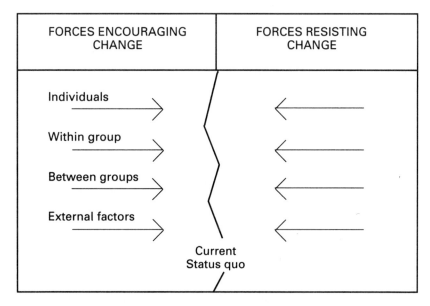

Figure 7.6 *Force field analysis*
Any position of status quo is the result of a balance between the various forces pushing for change and the elements of the reistance to change.
These various elements can be divided into the groups illustrated.

It suggests that change does not have to be total but that success can be achieved by shifting the balance towards the desired state.

For example, no company would expect to eliminate wastage even if that were a general aim. Improvement would be defined as a continued reduction in rates towards zero. The same would apply to the number of staff who ignore safety rules, etc.

The strength of force field analysis is that it allows complex situations to be broken down into simpler components, each of which can be addressed separately. This in turn allows the consultant and client to design an action plan to address and reduce the resisting forces which brings about the sought-after change. In general, increasing the pushing forces only serves to increase the resistance and is counter-productive.

For the in-house consultant the technique is doubly useful because it can be done, and often is, on the back of an envelope. It is a powerful way of helping clients visualize a discussion and seems to encourage suggestions and new ideas. Few managers in our experience seem able to resist picking up a pen, or snatching the consultant's, and adding their own ideas. The method is also useful for analysing the results of group brainstorming sessions and engendering discussion between the factions who may be on opposite sides of the 'wavy line'.

The best techniques to use are those which are simple, well known to the consultant, encourage the participation of the client and the staff and which present a picture or structure.

Pencil and paper diagrams and matrices fit these criteria well. None of the work we have discussed with trainers working in a consultancy role has required highly sophisticated methods of control or analysis to manage them. However such techniques may be valuable in analysing data collected, especially financial or resource utilization figures.

REFLECTIVE QUESTION 7.2

How do you manage several projects concurrently?

Case Study

Liz planned her time carefully as she had to meet the time constraints agreed with Jim as well as carry on with her other work. One of the things she was concerned about was the 'lecture' given her by Jean Wright, emphasizing the need for training intervention to be closely integrated with current and future Board strategy at the same time being measurable and at one with people's expectations now and in the future. This meant as far as she could see that she would have to rething immediately a lot of the basic assumptions on which the two-level management courses, 'Management I' and 'Management II' were based. The more she became buried in the intricacies of Jim Broadhurst's department the more she risked losing sight of the strategic picture.

Jean had meanwhile started to show some interest in the work Liz had been getting involved in and wanted to be kept posted on developments.

A date had now been agreed for the initial training. The pattern was to be three half days with the three supervisors almost in the form of a coaching plus discussion session. Jim hadn't liked the word seminar as seeming too academic.

Liz felt that the project, as she liked to call it, didn't need a steering committee or working party to oversee it. The number of people involved did not justify that. However, mindful of the need to carry people with her when trying to bring about a changed situation she arranged a regular short meeting with Jim and also kept her file up to date so she had something to refer to if asked.

Liz was able to see the supervisors individually but for not as long as she would have liked. She found that the encounter itself was important to build a good relationship and to promote confidence but it was difficult at the end to assess exactly what had been achieved.

A point that she had realized before but which now came home forcibly to her was that all these meetings were in a sense potential learning exercises for one if not for both parties, and in that way were all equally developmental. More and more the supervisors were asking her opinion about things to do with the job. They seemed to be less apathetic than before and a bit more enthusiastic about their work. But this meant that they came forward with more views about the organization of the work. Gone was the almost obsessive feeling that management should do something about improving the density of the window blinds, the staff situation, the time-keeping situation generally. More interest was shown now in what the supervisors could do about it.

Liz thought she knew some of the reasons for these changes but she hesitated as to whether all of them should be passed on to the manager. She also felt that she ought to have planned for the 'change of heart' on the part of the supervisors and taken it into consideration in thinking through how she could marshal all the forces available to bring about change in the department.

She now incorporated into her notes her version of a diagram showing the forces working for and against the success of the programme. It seemed very much a situation of needing to work within guidelines and agreed criteria, because the more issues inevitably came out the longer one stayed in there asking questions. The whole affair could become one of receding objectives, a slippery issue with no obvious beginning and end.

► PROGRAMME OF ACTION

Review of last chapter's action
If you have been able to try out the sequence of activity suggested in Chapter 6 you will now have some experience of gathering, analysing, and possibly presenting, data. You may have found, depending on the size of the project, that you can settle for a simple approach based on a few essentials. Stay with it. What is important is to apply the spirit of a disciplined approach as well as the appropriate key techniques. Through practice and review both can become instinctive.

Action for this chapter
You are now managing your project. The measure of your success as far as this Chapter is concerned, will rest on the extent that you organize, control and coordinate yourself and your resources through time. We suggest you take three key points from this Chapter eg, the project file, the project champion and the responsibility matrix, and try these out. Do they work for *you* on *your* project? How could you alter these points to make them more useful to you? Keep reviewing your experience if you can.

8 Skills and Techniques – Disengagement and Continuation

> SUMMARY <

In this chapter we consider some of the issues which arise after an assignment has been negotiated and implemented. We explore the reasons for disengagement emphasizing the necessity for the trainer to engage in other projects elsewhere and also for client managers to take on the responsibility for implementing change. Managers need to extend their role in this way, learning new skills in the process in order to cope with the challenges they are left with.

As we point out, the trainer will have a new developmental role. Active involvement is replaced by sporadic activation of the strings from a distance.

After reading through this chapter and working through the suggested tasks and applications, you should be able to:

- disengage from the consultancy assignment to the satisfaction of both parties
- maintain the relationship beyond the end of the project
- integrate, directly or indirectly, what has been achieved with current and future developments.

Few pieces of consultancy work will finish abruptly or necessarily come to a natural conclusion. There will always be new matters arising and issues surfacing as a result of the work carried out. But there must be a disengagment if the overall work load is to be effectively and responsibly managed.

> ### REFLECTIVE QUESTION 8.1
> How is the client's dependence on the trainer to be cast off?

Casting off the Client's Dependence

Perhaps you are working through a solution now in answer to this question. Once again we can hypothesize generally, but also develop a pragmatic and practical response in the actual situation. The first thing to bear in mind in whatever action you take is that it should ensure that the client has a sense of:

- continuing good relationships;
- value for money;
- achievement of objectives;
- future direction.

Continuing Good Relationships

This is essential for future work and for cooperation and help in projects elsewhere indirectly affecting the earlier client. It is also useful for credibility and reputation. Good as well as bad news travels fast. A good reputation is established perhaps slowly but is certainly lost quickly.

Value for Money

The client feels he or she has had a good deal, and value for money. Here perception is all important. How easy it is for us to say 'I did hardly anything ... I think I told them something they already knew ... they were more than halfway there to sorting it out for themselves.' Does it matter if they perceive what you have done and contributed as useful, successful and enhancing? Sometimes this is something we just have to remind ourselves to accept!

Achievement of Objectives

The original objectives have been achieved or, if not, a satisfactory compromise has been reached or acceptable reasons produced. Certainly this is central to success. The circle is closed and the loose ends tied. This means that unresolved issues are not left in the air or conveniently overlooked. It is rather like ticking off a list of items – we all like the feeling of a satisfactory conclusion.

Future Direction

An agreement is reached on how the section or department can autonomously carry on developing and building when the assignment and the direct involvement of the consultant comes to a close. The essence of a successful consultancy assignment is that the change brought about becomes an integral part of new procedures, new operations or new behaviours. These must be reinforced and consolidated. The only way that this will happen is that all concerned not only understand and agree the changes, but have the knowledge and ability to keep things going.

The Final Meeting

A great deal will hang on the final review meeting between the consultant and the client. This ought to be the time to summarize what has been achieved and estimate its success against the original objectives. It is the occasion to establish clearly what might be termed 'forward looks'. This will also encompass:

- what remains to be done within the original brief;
- what new events or situations are likely to occur which will require some response;
- who is responsible for future project management;
- what is the likely role of the consultant in the future.

Establishing a Link Person

One idea which might be applicable, especially where the project has been of a sufficient size or other developments are likely to occur, is that of identifying a 'link person' on site who in fact takes on the former role of the consultant trainer. This person will be useful as an intermediary on a permanent basis from whom and to whom the trainer can feed in the future. What will happen is that, with a number of projects and the passage of time, learning proceeds on a parallel basis with individual change. In this way, learning and change become more of a collective group or organizational process.

The trainer's role adapts and changes perhaps in the direction we suggest in Chapter 9.

Maintaining Relationships

As we have already discussed, good working relationships are essential to the successful negotiation and implementation of a consultancy project.

Good relationships, which means having confidence in the other people and their ability and respect for their positions and experience, will encourage the effective use of interpersonal skills, the free flow of data as well as engendering an atmosphere where cooperation is most likely to take place. Another advantage is that political interplay, ie jockeying for position and prestige, covert communication, hidden agenda and multiple objectives, are less likely to interfere with the exchange of facts, views and opinions. A climate is created where frank interchanges can take place and teamwork can thrive. Motivation goes hand in hand with a culture which values people's experience and contributions.

REFLECTIVE QUESTION 8.2

How can effective working relationships be maintained beyond the end of the project?

Once the project has been brought to a conclusion, which will be helped if the criteria within the contract terms have been clear, a good working relationship does not require such frequent personal contact. Of course there will be things the consultant can do. Agreeing to 'call in' at set times or dates, attending to residual matters, making an effort to ask informally about progress and developments, will all help. Another idea is that of making contact through other people or some subject matter. This is the food and drink of normal communication. Indirect contact and mentions of interest through intermediaries are also useful. Probably most vital is the positive and practical close to the assignment. This leaves a strong message which is retained for a long time. People like it when others show interest in their concerns, especially when they have something practical to offer.

Matching Assignments to Operational and Strategic Requirements

It is likely that you have sold your services as a contribution to skills and knowledge enhancement, ie what most people would regard as training with or without the development which we would see going hand in hand. Possibly you have now started to market the concept of performance improvement and behavioural change as being the hallmark of your contribution to organizational effectiveness.

Eventually, as in the case of most trainers, you will most likely want your efforts to be associated with improvements to the organization as a whole, bringing about change which is closely linked to day-to-day operations. In other words, training is not set aside in a watertight compartment as a sort of nice but optional extra. Rather it is closely tied in with every other aspect of the business, whatever that may be. This is something to strive for. The more we can make links between what we offer and all the other concerns of the client, the more we can prove the worth of our services. The training function as a whole will gain enormously in reputation and credibility. This means using the right language, it means the trainer being steeped in business activities and all the other activities of the client. Links can be made in conversation, at review meetings, in the feedback reports. However, tread carefully. Like everything else it is a matter of balance. You cannot have an exhaustive knowledge of the client's business, but as an internal consultant you work for the same organization. You have common concerns, an inside view, an empathy even which the external consultant cannot hope to match. However you will not wish to be given all sorts of extra 'unofficial' tasks just because you are perceived as keen, informed and motivated to help. Nor do you wish to arouse hostility, suspicion and resentment by appearing to take over the manager's job. Many trainers will continue to fall into this trap if they are not sensitive to people and situations as well as their own limitations.

REFLECTIVE QUESTION 8.3

How can extra 'unofficial' tasks be avoided?

This is a situation you may already have come across. It is not just a question of saying 'no' prefaced by 'sorry'! Better to refer to the contract agreement, point out the context of the assignment in relation to your role and workload as a whole. If there could be something here which you think falls within your brief, agree to come back to discuss it. Arrange a date and time. Again, as always, be positive, task-related and specific. You are unlikely, or less likely, to offend.

Case Study

When the supervisors' sessions had taken place, with one or two adjustments to cover for the enforced absence of one of them, everyone including Liz seemed to be quite pleased with the result. The supervisors were able to put forward their plans to Jim for training of their own staff as well as their views and reactions to some of the other issues raised affecting the way work was carried out in the department. Jim's staff meetings seemed to be more purposeful, particularly as he started to feed back to the staff more of what was happening in the organization as a whole.

He now started talking to Liz about other areas of training that he professed interest in. He mentioned, for example, more on budgets, time management, health and safety, updates on office equipment, word processing systems.

Although the way she had originally negotiated her services and time had not been as 'tight' as she would have ideally liked, Liz nevertheless found that the principles that had been originally agreed as well as the objectives of the project now provided a good lever in bringing her involvement to a close.

Reviewing her forces for change diagram she proposed to Jim the following:

Jim would agree priority training areas for the supervisors through the normal staff meetings. The topics would be set against the departmental objectives now being clarified. Additionally the supervisors would be asked to define performance standards using the models that had been already learned. He could consult Liz on any problem when this had been done.

Jim would also clarify what help he wanted from the full-time trainers when he was ready but he would also put forward a plan showing what was to be achieved by when in a particular time frame. This plan must include a specific statement on what the department would be doing for themselves.

Liz would agree to talk to Jim on a month-to-month basis to remain in touch. This was deliberately kept firm but vague. After discussion with Jean, Liz wanted to avoid being seen by Jim as constantly on call as a perpetual consultant trainer to his workforce.

This assignment went into the annual report of the Training Department as an internal document used to ascertain how resources had been used and to what effect. Added to it were some generalities about what had been learned from the assignment taken from Liz Clarke's file as maintained by her.

► PROGRAMME OF ACTION ◄

Review of last chapter's action

By now, if you have stayed with each chapter, you will have been engaged in at least one consultancy assignment. You will have set up a contract or working agreement. You will have made relationships, involved people in order to carry them with you, implemented an action plan and hopefully have moved or are moving to a successful conclusion. How do you stand now? Has it been worth the effort?

Very likely you will have found that things have taken longer to do than you planned and there have been lots of untidy strands which ideally needed tidying up on the way. Equally likely you will have found some short cuts and things we haven't mentioned which worked well for you. You have to finish the project with other work and projects pressing. Maybe you are finding yourself a victim of your own success.

Action for this chapter

Consider your current consultancy assignment, or one you can reasonably identify with at least hypothetically. Draft some notes for the final review meeting, covering future activities, what needs doing and who should do it. Ensure the four criteria outlined above can be observed.

Review some of your past work with managers and identify those actions which fall into the category of disengagement. Did any of your work suffer from lack of closing actions?

This is really the end of your experience of consultancy as an in-house trainer. It leaves us with tasks of disengaging from the assignment, withdrawing positively, but leaving the door open so we can go back and be welcomed. We also have to ensure that developments don't stop. We cannot be seen as so helpful, so expert, that nothing will happen unless we do it or pull the strings. If we have been successful things will go on happening. Word will reach you, the trainer, to let you know of changes and developments.

In practical terms, now is the time to reflect on your experiences. You could list some of the problems and difficulties you have encountered, how you responded, what results you got and what remains to be done.

9 Consultancy for Tomorrow

▷   SUMMARY   ◁

In the following chapter we explain our vision of the future for training consultancy, both internal and external, over the next 10 to 15 years.

We describe the current trends in the market for training services, the changing roles and increasing concentration on process skills needed by practitioners, how better evaluation is leading to outcome-based payment systems (no change – no charge) and the increasing demand for credible and relevant qualifications.

We consider the impact these changes will have on the practice of external consultant and how this will in turn impact on the work of internal consultants who will need to compare themselves with such outsiders.

After reading this chapter you should be able to:

- identify future prospects for trainers working in a consultancy style
- consolidate your learning
- speculate at dinner parties with the best of them.

In Chapter 2 we examined current changes in the training scene and in Chapter 4, the alterations needed in organizations to promote the development of a consultancy approach. Now we shall extrapolate these observations and try to identify their implications. Much of this will be speculation but we hope that the future we paint will be one that will inspire trainers to add consultancy skills to their repertoire and shift their way of working towards that of the in-house trainer as consultant.

The New Training Market

The current trend for experienced trainers to become self-employed and work throughout their industry looks set to continue. As training consultants become more widespread there will be increased specialization in their roles, expertise will become deeper and narrower, extra hands will have to be available at shorter notice and at the exact times required by the manager, and interpersonal skills will need to become even more sharply honed. (We have a nightmare of the science fiction 'empath' with the ability to read minds and feelings. The nearest things so far are the superstar 'gurus' travelling the world spreading the gospel!)

Such specialization will require very sophisticated information systems and cooperative registers to enable clients to identify suitable, available assistance. Qualification or endorsement systems will need to be much more exact than at present, being capable of giving clients a reliable, consistent statement of the trainer's abilities. Moves towards a chartered status for consultants will become irresistible. A new industry will grow up to train and assess the competence of consultants. The identity and experience of assessors will be a delicate matter to decide. There will be much opportunity for people currently in the system to set themselves up as the 'experts'.

These events will be of importance to in-house consultants since they will need to be able to compare themselves with the services offered by those operating outside their organization. They will need to convince managers of their credibility and likelihood to succeed.

More and more trainers will find themselves working in collaboration with outsiders. This will be an opportunity to learn and develop. It will also be an opportunity for strife and conflict. As an internal trainer you may compare yourself with the outsider and wonder why you are not getting the same fee or recognition. If internal trainers are trying to adopt a consultancy style then outsiders will become competitors in every sense of the term. There is a real risk that the marvellous characteristic of all trainers to share experience with each other will be lost. This would be a real shame since it would run counter to the espoused intention to develop a learning relationship. It would also reduce the enjoyment to be had at work and in trainer networks.

REFLECTIVE QUESTION 9.1

How can you build on and extend the consultancy role?

Pay and Rewards

Pay

The emphasis in judging training success is rapidly moving towards measurement of outcomes. It seems likely that the pay of trainers may be decided in the same way. The days of time plus profit contracts are numbered. We have already seen the start of this in the UK with the funding arrangements for youth training linked to successful outcomes in national vocational qualifications for participants. Health Authority contracts with colleges of nursing, physiotherapy, etc, will pay for the number of qualified staff leaving, not as at present, on the number of entrants. Some consultancies are asking no guaranteed fee but an agreed percentage of increases in company profits.

We foresee that 'no change – no charge' contracts may become the rule. The level of fee could be determined by some measure of individual or company performance. Other measures could include the number of relevant competences acquired, the extent to which individual development plans are met or some measure of 'added value' to individual employees. We have already seen discussion papers on transfer fees for individuals being calculated (much as for sports stars); this would be an interesting way to calculate payment for the coach!

Intrinsic rewards

The rewards for trainers as consultants will also shift from leading groups in creative activities or the buzz of helping individuals to learn some aspect of their job, to helping managers improve the performance of their department. The shift is not a great one but learning to recognize the new, less immediate, indicators of success may be.

Information Systems

Within organizations the information systems will need to be developed to cope with capturing and recording what are essentially opportunistic learning experiences. Annual review systems will need to be supplemented by end-of-event reviews designed to reinforce learning and to build up the organization's knowledge about its own capacity and flexibility. Again the first signs of such developments are being seen with databases designed to record staff assessments against national or local competence schemes. The internal consultant may decide on appropriate interventions on the basis of gaps in the organization's skills or competence profiles kept in this way.

The grapevine of managerial gossip and reputation will start to hum with the news of who can be relied on to help the learning of individuals and groups. Not a general topic of conversation at the moment!

REFLECTIVE QUESTION 9.2

What are the difficulties caused by a successful track record?

Structure of the Training Function

The need for structured training events for groups of staff with similar, predictable learning requirements will remain in many organizations. We would not suggest that the typical Training Department will become redundant. Whatever structure and skill mix is currently relevant will be augmented by specific members of staff acting as full-time consultants. Or, perhaps more effective, each member of the training staff will include a consultancy style and repertoire of skills in their role. The most mature development of this scheme will be displayed when the line managers of the organization have such roles built into their job descriptions to assist colleagues and staff to develop and learn.

Staff Skills

The principal shift will be towards greater self-awareness among all staff of the way they behave at work and the effect this has on others. Improved communication skills and interpersonal sensitivity will be demanded. This is not to say that the way forward is all gentleness, consideration and enlightened managerial behaviour. Such skills can be used to exploit and manipulate staff as at present. We merely suggest that the level of sophistication of the processes involved will become higher. This in turn puts extra demands on the process consultant to stay one step ahead of the clientele.

As trainers need to act more as consultants, perhaps paid on results, they will need to improve the business skills they deploy to run their department. The training function may well become a profit centre for the organization, judged according to the same rules as their clients are judged by. This will put pressure on to work where most money can be made. Calculated risks will need to be taken and evaluated. Should the trainer go for currently profitable departments to ride on their cash or seek to assist loss-making departments for a share in increased income? The ability to make such judgement is still rare among trainers.

Changes to Organizational Culture

It is currently in vogue to talk of the development of the learning organization. One in which learning, rather than training, is emphasized; where learning carries on throughout employment in response to the changing demands of the external environment and the internal motivations of staff. The UK Institute of Training and Development has committed itself to the development of a 'learning world' in its mission statement.

Such pervasive changes to the perceptions of working life will take a lot of effort to bring about. Few trainers have come to terms with what that means for their department, profession and methods of working. One thing is certain: it will not be achieved by corporate training courses on the development of a learning organization!

It seems to us that trainers must adopt a greater role as change agents, specializing in catalysing changes in individual and group behaviours, based on a sound understanding of the learning process.

Conclusion

In our experience most in-house trainers include some elements of consultancy in their work. They don't give it any fancy airs or titles; they just work with people in their place of work to bring about beneficial changes. More and more are working in a project-based mode. We have tried to bring out the various skills and techniques needed, and the organizational and political changes which are being imposed on these activities, and have tried to describe how they can best be harnessed by individual trainers. This last chapter unashamedly goes a little beyond the evidence to try to look into the future and help people prepare.

We hope that having read through the book and carried out some of the tasks the role of in-house consultancy has been demystified, and that we have enabled you to adopt those parts which best suit your current situation.

▶ PROGRAMME OF ACTION ◀

Review of last chapter's action
Reviewing the end of some of your past assignments may have been a little uncomfortable. Did they have a recognizable finish, or did they just peter out? Was the future input to the department agreed? Did you summarize and reinforce the learning achieved by the staff involved and yourself? Unless these actions are taken at the end of a piece of work much of its benefits to the organization are lost and the participants are often left with a feeling of confusion or resentfulness. This last point is especially important with individuals who have provided data or been interviewed. At the very least each should be contacted and thanked and if possible a short summary of the benefits to their department circulated. Such sensitivity to the needs of staff is a good sign that the in-house trainer is likely to succeed as a consultant.

Action for this chapter
Start planning the next consultancy assignment. Go back through the chapters in this book. Pick out the practical offerings and highlight those you can best use next time round and which best suit your particular circumstance. We can but wish you good fortune. Perhaps, like us, you see the future of training and its inevitable move towards consultancy work – with all that the concept and term implies – as an exciting and rewarding one. At least we hope you will improve your satisfaction, your feeling of self-progression and survival prospects.

Appendix 1

Case Study – Jackie Marsh

The Background

Jean McCracken had just started in post as the Director of Personnel for the newly-formed Trust status hospital. She had been brought in from a large contract catering and hotel chain to add some experience of private sector personnel work to the well-established Personnel Department. David James, the previous Unit Personnel Manager, had applied unsuccessfully for the job but was making a good fist of helping Jean into the workings of the NHS. Jean was describing to David the proceedings at the most recent Executive Board Meeting she had attended.

'They want to introduce a new appraisal scheme, less bureaucratic than the National Scheme. It's got to have a real 'Trust' look as part of our separate corporate identity policy.'

David wasn't really listening, he knew it was coming and dreaded the extra amount of work. It was all piling up, especially with the new contracts and negotiating systems he was working on. 'Can't we get someone in to do it?' he moaned.

'The Chief Executive suggested someone called Jackie Marsh from District. What do you know about her?'

'Jackie's OK. She's been in the District for years, made a good job of closing the old geriatric hospital and now runs popular courses. I don't know what she knows about appraisal though. Besides, do we really want someone from 'District' snooping around and telling us what to do?'

No formal cross-charging system had been set up between District and Trusts so Jackie's services would be free if she could be persuaded to do the job. Since funds were very tight that decided it.

'David, you know her, can you explain what we want and ask her to help? I would also like your advice on setting up a small working party to get things going. Who do you suggest?'

'Oh,' pondered David, 'the Director of Nursing Practice, the Head of Therapies, Director of Finance for pay implications, the Quality Assurance Manager, someone from Estates Management, yourself and Jackie, oh! and don't forget Pathology and the Labs.'

This was in fact the usual group of people who oversaw most policy-making decisions, although since the Trust had been re-structured only the Estates Manager and the Head of Pathology actually managed a group of staff. All the others were now in advisory and monitory roles with just 2 or 3 assistants.

'What about the clinical heads of Surgery, Medicine and Elderly Care?' asked Jean.

'They won't want to get involved, they have their work cut out keeping the place going'.

Briefing Jackie Marsh

David and Jackie met the following week. 'Oh come on Jackie!' said David. 'You know the situation as well as I do. Bill [the Trust Chief Executive] wants a new system, we all want to get rid of the old paperwork, you've said yourself that it gets in the way on training courses.'

'That's all very well, but what are you looking for in its place? It's no good coming up with one half-baked idea – that's worse than the old scheme.'

'That's for you to find out. We've set up a working party to look at the design of the new system and we'd like you to facilitate their work. Then you'll need to implement the scheme and train the staff to use it.'

Jackie looked unconvinced by David's explanations of what was needed. 'Look,' she said, 'I'll speak to Bill and a few of the others and draw up the objectives of the programme and the likely features of any final scheme. If I think I can help I'll write out a timetable, a sort of proposal if you like, and we can take it from there.'

Jackie arranged to speak to as many of those involved as possible, mostly over the phone but to Bill and the Director of Nursing Practice face to face.

The main points were that:

1. Bill wanted to create a sense of identity and purpose in the new organization, emphasizing quality of care and professionalism.
2. The current system was used by all the senior managers (25 people) and was linked to about 5 per cent performance-related pay.
3. The forms covered all the necessary ground but were poorly laid out and difficult to complete, especially with word processors.
4. Performance review was used extensively on the therapists and radiographers (who had their own system) but virtually nowhere else.
5. The Estates Manager was concerned about its effect on the current complex bonus schemes.
6. Any new system would have to be compatible with the requirements of the current senior managers' contracts which had to have a 1–5 grading for pay purposes.

Jackie Gets Involved

Jackie knew the scheme well. It was a management-by-objective system in which work objectives were set, with key actions and success criteria. These were reviewed on a more or less regular basis and formally once a year when an overall rating of 1–5 was given to determine performance-related pay.

The associated system of training-needs analysis and career discussion was used hardly at all. It had degenerated into a paper chase in some departments.

Many of the nurses associated performance appraisal with old-style trait analyses (rating 'enthusiasm' or 'dress sense' from A to E!) used in their student days. They didn't relish coming back for more!

Jackie wrote a fairly detailed description of the position as she saw it, giving prominence to Bill's overall vision of an organizational development initiative, a new simpler system to encourage excellent performance throughout the new Trust.

Reading it through again she became quite excited by the possibilities of the project and saw an easily transferred product for other Units.

She popped the final document into the post with an air of expectation.

The Project Group Meets

The first meeting of the project group was a shambles.

Jean did not want to take the chair because she was too new in post and insisted Jackie chair this and all subsequent meetings. There was no secretary to take any minutes and none of the participants volunteered. The Estates Manager sent apologies and the Director of Finance sent the Head of Purchasing in his place.

The meeting started off as a long series of moans about the old system except from the Head of Therapies who thought it perfectly OK. She only wanted a programme of training and implementation to spread its use throughout the Trust. She certainly did not want to undermine all the work her staff had invested to make the system function. It was up to the others to catch up.

The only real business that had been achieved was that a time and venue had been agreed for the next meeting. (That was only due to the suggestion of the Head of Purchasing).

Afterwards Jackie was cross that she had prepared the ground so badly and been forced into the chair. It had never occurred to her that anyone would arrange a meeting with no agenda! At least if she took the chair that kind of thing wouldn't happen again. It was some weeks before she was to discover the real difficulties of this position.

> ### REFLECTIVE QUESTION A.1.1
>
> What are these problems likely to be?

Jackie's Report

Despite tight, clearly expressed agendas, two more meetings produced no progress in defining suitable objectives for the new appraisal scheme. Finally Jackie offered to write an option appraisal report outlining the alternatives and their various pros and cons. The group could then decide on one option.

Jackie got stuck into the work with gusto. At least now some progress could be made. She collected examples of different systems from a wide variety of sources, arranged interviews with a carefully selected group of staff and managers and compared each system against a checklist of desirable and undesirable features. She experimented with a weighted variable decision-making method but abandoned it as too complex to explain.

All her work pointed to a simplification of the present system as the way forward with reprinted, more elegant and less detailed forms. They all needed to be reprinted in the Trust's new colours and logo anyway so it was the ideal time to make the changes.

If the first three meetings of the project group had been merely unproductive, the fourth, and final, one was quite spiteful.

'I don't know why you bothered with this group at all,' said one. 'It's obvious you've made your mind up what you want to do whatever we say.'

'I thought you were working for us,' said another, 'not us for you.'

Jackie was shaken. It was a good piece of work; she had shown it to colleagues who had been impressed by its clarity and fairness. Yes, they had agreed with all her recommendations. She didn't know how to wind this group up or reach any agreement.

In the end the committee agreed to call it a draft report and sent it to the Executive Board without any recommendations.

After the meeting two of the people phoned Jackie to apologize about how she had been treated.

The Executive Board considered the report and resolved to simplify the current system 'in line with option three which seems clearly the one most likely to succeed'.

Conclusion

This was the state of affairs when Jackie met some colleagues from other Districts in a learning network that they had set up to support and challenge each other's progress. They convinced her that she couldn't leave it there. Even if she didn't sort it out with the project group she ought to talk it through with the Chief Executive.

Jackie phoned Bill and asked for an opportunity to discuss the project with him. She was not looking forward to the meeting one bit. She felt that as the consultant she ought to explain – indeed to account for – what had happened in the group, but she really wanted Bill's advice on how she could have done it. The roles were reversed and she felt a fraud.

At the meeting Bill congratulated her on her report and thanked her for her work. He had heard that the project group had not been very productive. He wanted to talk through why Jackie thought that was. What lessons could they learn about handling projects in the future ...

Appendix 2

Case Study – David Williams

Background

David Williams is a Personnel and Training Manager. He works for the distribution arm of a large electronics and electrical manufacturer. He has a long work record with them – eight years – and was a prominent figure during a difficult trading period when 15 per cent of the workforce was made redundant. His considerate handling of exit interviews, and common sense approach to staffing issues during subsequent realignments and growth, have left him with a good reputation across the firm.

David values his links with the Personnel Department. They provide him with good information on what is going on, access to the Board through his director and strong working links with managers during regular recruitment and selection, and work performance issues. His consultancy style for training work is unashamedly opportunist, picking up on snippets of information, following them through and caring, on a personal level, about how people in the firm are getting on. 'If I didn't care about the people, I wouldn't be able to work in this way,' he once confided.

The case study we will follow with David was a spin-off from part of a review his Department was carrying out into the role and function of the Sales Department.

Securing the Contract

'What the hell do these people think their job is?'

This was turning into a difficult telephone conversation between David and the head of the Southern Sales Department, Ian Riggs. It had all started with an excellent report defining the jobs and perceptions of roles of people throughout the sales division, so why had Ian decided to pick out the section on sales support and admin. staff to get so hot under the collar? There were only six of them.

'Ian,' David soothed him, 'I can see this is a problem for you, can I come and see you, or meet for lunch to talk it through? OK, OK, I'll come up now.'

A few moments later in Ian's office David was wishing he hadn't arrived so quickly. Ian was still angry with the report, blaming Personnel for putting daft ideas 'into his girls' heads' and then 'presenting the whole thing as if that was how it was *supposed* to be'.

David too was getting cross. The results were based on questionnaires to the individuals, backed up by standard interviews carried out by freelance consultants. They were good and reliable, their observations agreed with his own knowledge of what the staff did, with the job descriptions on file and their supervisor's definition of what she thought the staff should do. 'All he wants to do is rubbish my department because he doesn't like the results,' thought David.

Relating the story later, David described how he saw this building into an argument but caught himself just in time. He wanted to cool the conversation quickly and direct Ian from his attacks on the report and the Personnel Department and find out what had triggered Ian's obvious annoyance.

Consciously deciding not to defend anything, David listened and listened some more. As Ian ran out of steam David interjected more often, asking a question, reflecting back comments, until he said, 'I can see you are angry, but from what you have said I don't think it's with the report. What's the problem?'

The problem was real enough, personal and nothing to do with work. David listened some more, offered no advice and left on reasonably good terms.

Two days later David phoned Ian. 'Ian, you know that job description problem with the sales administration people, I'd like to follow it up. Word has it that you're in a better temper – is it safe to come and talk?'

'Don't be so bloody silly, of course its OK,' said Ian, 'I'm sorry about losing my temper, it wasn't you, you know how it is. Look, I know I was over the top, but they really don't have the right idea about what they should be doing. I'd like to sort it out. Make an appointment through my secretary.'

> ## REFLECTIVE QUESTION A.2.1
>
> How would you prepare for the interview?

Establishing the Parameters

'The sales clerks see their role as dealing with customer complaints and queries and to process orders in the normal way. They chase the progress of orders in response to enquiries from customers or sales staff. A lot of their work seems to be taking down orders placed by phone either following visits from sales staff or from people calling direct. Much of the work is repeat orders for consumables,' David explains.

'I know all that,' said Ian, 'but we have a warehouse full of stock. Why don't they try selling it? They have eager customers, many long established. It's is not like cold calling. Not one of them, or their bloody supervisor, even mentions 'selling goods' as part of their job. They just see themselves as takers of dictation and form fillers. I want them selling the stuff.'

'Let me get this straight,' said David. He entered into a fairly detailed discussion, trying to define what additional behaviours Ian was expecting of the staff. They talked it through for half-an-hour, David listening and summarizing at regular intervals. He reflected back Ian's concerns about how to introduce the changes he wanted and how to deal with the supervisor, who clearly didn't see eye to eye with him on the role of this group and had encouraged and entrenched them into a very bureaucratic method of working.

By the end of the conversation they had agreed that David would draw up a confidential new job description, including the elements of work that Ian wanted to be included. He would also examine the implications for pay and conditions for the administrative staff, any effects it might have on commissions for the field sales staff, and the training needs it might bring up. He would not speak to any sales staff at the moment.

David had persuaded Ian that he and the section supervisor should put the idea to the group after the three of them had discussed the issues and prepared the presentation. David would not be present so as not to divert attention or give the impression it was a 'Personnel inspired' idea. He would be available to discuss the training issues after their meeting.

David wrote up his notes after the meeting, emphasizing who would do what, with a few suggested dates (they hadn't been agreed at the time) and sent a copy to Ian and his Director. One week later he submitted a two-page report on the financial implications of the job amendments, possible knock-on effects to other staff, and likely training needs based on the experience of the staff involved. He appended a new draft job description.

Preparing the Ground

David met Sue (the supervisor) and Ian about a week before they were due to speak to their staff. He had made a mental list of the points he wanted to cover with them. How do you intend to handle this? Who will say what? Where have you arranged to meet them? How will they set it out? How much say do they have in their future? Must all the staff work in the new way? Will you pay them more? How will the customers react?

He felt well prepared and was convinced that Ian was right. These people could have a significant impact on sales if handled properly.

The meeting didn't go as David would have liked. Sue looked resentful, contributing very little other than criticisms of suggestions or snappy sarcasm of the modest financial incentives Ian was offering. After the meeting broke up David tackled Ian about it. 'Sue seemed quite antagonistic. Are you sure you have got her on board?'

Ian was silent.

David waited, the pause seemed very uncomfortable. 'She didn't agree,' said Ian, 'I overruled her and said we should go ahead anyway.'

David waited again. 'Oh, I know I was wrong, but I just don't have the time to nanny everyone around to my way of thinking. Sometimes it's better just to pitch in and see if it works.'

David looked thoughtful and asked, 'How much time will you have to spend on this if you don't have Sue's support?'

Ian looked down at his desk and nodded.

'Don't do your naughty schoolboy act now,' joked David. 'What's in it for her if this goes through, and why is she so against the whole idea?'

'Will you speak to her, David?'

'No, I don't think so,' said David. 'You and Sue need to work it out and develop a better understanding. I'll go through it with you now if you like, but I really think you should talk to her.'

Ian knew well enough what needed to be done, but seemed to

have some sort of block. David spent a few minutes trying to find out what it was, picking up on Ian's concerns. At the end of the discussion David still didn't really know what the problem was. Back in his office the phone rang. It was Sue. 'David, I want to talk to you privately about this selling business, have you got a moment?'

REFLECTIVE QUESTION A.2.2–4

How would you handle this?
Who is your client?
What kind of contract/relationship do you have with Sue?

David decided to take a small risk and listen to Sue's problems over the phone. Thankfully it all seemed fairly straightforward. She was anxious about managing a group of sales staff when she herself had only ever been in administration. She just 'knew' that some of the younger staff would be much better at it than her. She was worried about her status and ability to cope. David tried to reassure Sue that she could cope and that she was worrying needlessly. 'Have you spoken to Ian about this?' he asked.

Sue paused for a long time. 'Oh,' she said, 'I can't talk to him. He doesn't listen like you do.'

David was flattered, he knew Sue was right, but said, 'Oh, I wouldn't say that. Ian is very considerate. I know he would like to talk it through with you. If you don't tell him how you feel what's it going to be like over the next few weeks? I know you can sort it out.'

Soon after the staff meeting Ian phoned David to tell him how it went. He had been pleased, two of the staff had had similar ideas but hadn't said anything before. This helped sway the others. No one even asked about extra money, so when Ian had said, 'Of course there will be a little commission to be earned,' it had come as a bonus. Sue tells him that the office is alive with jokes about travelling salesmen. She thinks the laughter has more to do with nerves than the quality of the jokes.

All the staff agreed that they wanted training in telesales techniques and product knowledge. Ian asked David to 'set something up' for them, which he agreed to do.

'By the way,' said Ian, 'What did you say to Sue?'

'Well, nothing really, why?' asked David. 'Did she do well?'

'Oh, nothing. Thanks, goodbye'.

David summarized the telephone call as 'terms of reference' for the next phase of the work. He prepared a short memo to Ian, copied to Sue, on how he would identify the training needs with the staff concerned, with an estimation of when it would be finished and when the training could start. It seemed like an ideal job for Hilary, the sales trainer.

The Next Phase

David has worked with Ian and Sue to brief the sales administration staff on their increased telesales role. He has asked Hilary to work with the sales staff to train them in the necessary skills.

Over lunch in the canteen David asked Hilary how the training of the sales administrators was progressing.

'It's going really well,' said Hilary. 'They had a lot of ideas about what they wanted. I used some methods I learnt at my last job. To be honest, they were so keen I didn't have to do very much. We set up a monitoring system on sales of video tapes to customers ordering video recorders and post the results. It's really cut-throat, but very good humoured. Sue was a bit of a problem. I've had to work hard with her, but it seems OK. I've done virtually everything I agreed with Ian. The trouble is, I can't tell if he's pleased with progress or not. We're ahead of any sort of sales targets we set (they were hopelessly low), but he hasn't said anything to me.'

'Why don't you ask him ...?' ventured David.

Conclusion

David had followed progress largely at a distance. A comment here, a remark there, often during a squash game with Ian, or like this with Hilary.

Eight weeks after the staff meeting David received a copy of Hilary's final report. It had obviously gone well. David was pleased. He jotted a note on the cover and passed it to his Director 'for information', noting that the initiative would probably work well in the other regions of the firm. 'Sound out the boss and see if he would like us to offer it around.'

He made some mental notes about future work with Ian. Why do two fairly assertive members of staff find him difficult and unresponsive? Am I going to feed this back sometime, and how?

He phoned Sue. 'Hello, Sue. I've read Hilary's report on the training work. Well done. Why don't you write it up for the house magazine, it would make a change to hear some good news. And what about you, how are you finding it ...?'

Appendix 3

Related Reading

This is not an academic work and we have not sought to make endless references to other published work in this field. However, in trying out in-house training consultancy on a practical basis, we feel readers' learning and effectiveness will be enhanced by a modicum of literature search.

Not everyone has the time to read extensively. However, we feel a sight of several of the following will reinforce what we have written – and inspire or promote or satisfy the desire to learn (and do) more. The list includes authors to whom we have referred in the text.

Bennett, R (ed.) (1988) *Improving Trainer Effectiveness*, Gower. (Papers dealing with how the role of trainers is developing and can develop.)

Bennis, W G (1969) *Organisation Development: Its Nature, Origins and Prospects*, Addison-Wesley.

Clark, N (1991) *Managing Personal Learning and Change*, McGraw Hill.

Dickson, A (1982) *A Woman in Your Own Right*, Quartet Books.

Galbraith, J (1973) *Designing Complex Organisations*, Addison-Wesley.

Handy, C (1985) *The Future of Work*, Blackwell. (Inspiring background analysis of the world of employment work and significant developments.)

Kearsley, G (1982) *Costs, Benefits and Productivity in Training Systems*, Addison-Wesley.

Kolb, D A, Rubin, I M, McIntyre, J M (1974) *Organizational Psychology, a Book of Readings*, 2nd edition Prentice Hall.

Kotler, P (1976) *Marketing Management*, Prentice hall.

Lewin, K (1947) 'Group decisions and social change' *in* Newcomb, T & Harltley E (Eds) *Readings in Social Psychology*, Holt, Rinehart & Winston.

Lockyer, K G (1964) *An Introduction to Critical Path Analysis*, Pitman.

Mager ,R and Pipe, P (1991) *Analysing Performance Problems*, Kogan Page.

Margerison, C J (1988) *Managerial Consulting Skills*, Gower. (A detailed analysis of a whole range of skills and models of consultancy.)

Manpower Services Commission Direct Trainers (1980) *2nd Report of the Training of Trainers Committee* HMSO.

Phillips, K and Shaw, P (1989) *A Consultancy Approach for Trainers*, Gower. (An excellent and detailed survey of the need for and practice of the internal consultancy role.)

Walton, M (1986) 'Training for change: a case study of the trainer's role' *Journal of European Industrial Training*, 10, C.

The suggested reading and references in these publications will suggest further sources of study.

A whole range of offerings are on the market to help trainers and others develop their consultancy skills. Examples are:

Consulting and Influencing Skills for Internal Advisors	Oxford Management Consultants 29 Western Road Henley-on-Thames Oxon RG9 1JN
Trainer into Consultant	Brunel Management Programme Brunel University Uxbridge Middlesex UB8 3PH
Consultancy Skills	Shepard Moscow Ltd Orpington Kent BR7 5DA

Index